BLUEPRINT OF LEADERSHIP

TO GET FROM WHERE YOU ARE TO WHERE YOU NEED TO BE

THIRTEEN STEPS TO MANUFACTURE SUCCESS

NICK JARMAN

Ordering Information:
Quantity Sales: Special discounts are available on quantity purchases by corporations, associations, and others. For details, contact the publisher at the email address above.

ISBN: 978-0-578-74224-3
Library of Congress Control Number (LCCN): 2020914675

Front and back cover book design by Sonu Parmar
Back cover image by Dena McDonald, Orange Light Studios
Printed in the United States of America.

First printing edition 2020.

Website: www.nickmjarman.com

Leadership, Leader, Business, Entrepreneurship, Brand, Success, Communication

Contents

INTRODUCTION

YOUR SHOPPING CART

You know when you are at the grocery store, and you see shopping carts littered around the parking lot? That is something that has always personally driven me insane. Maybe it has to do with the countless hours I spent working at a grocery store growing up gathering these shopping carts during my high-school years. Just recently I received a text message with an image of a shopping cart, and it said, "you can't be successful until you learn to put your shopping cart away." At first glance I simply laughed, but then my mind started to think of how true that really is.

I started to realize there are in fact two different types of people in this world: cart returners and cart deserters. Whichever group you stand with says a lot about you. The shopping cart is the ultimate litmus test for whether a person is capable of self-governing. To return the shopping cart is an easy, convenient task and one which we all recognize as the correct, appropriate thing to do.

To return the shopping cart is objectively right. There are no situations other than dire emergencies in which a person is not able to return their cart. At the same time, it is not illegal to abandon your shopping cart. Therefore, the shopping cart presents itself as the peak example of whether a person will do what is right without being forced to do it. No one will punish you for not returning the shopping cart, no one will fine you or kill you for not returning the shopping cart, you gain nothing by returning the shopping cart.

CART RETURNERS PUT OTHERS FIRST

There are countless excuses for someone to leave their cart propped up on a grassy median or left between parking spaces. Maybe they are in a hurry to get home before dinner or it is pouring rain outside. Maybe they are trying to escape the dirty looks they are getting because their oversized truck is parked across two spaces. Whatever the reason is, there is one thing all these excuses have in common: it is all about them.

When you take the time to return your cart to its receptacle, you are showing that you care about the employees of the grocery store. You care about the baggers, stock clerks, cashier's, manager, etc. You acknowledge that if you do not put the cart away, someone else will have to do it for you. Basically, it shows that you are not a selfish person. Why not take it a step further? If you see someone needing help with a cart, offer to return it for them. It is all about helping our neighbor, helping each other.

You see, successful people put others first. Instead of being wrapped up in things that benefit them, they look for ways to help and serve those around them. Because when it comes to life you will get what you want, if you help enough other people get what they want. Simply put, it is called servant leadership. The simple goal of servant leadership is to serve.

Take for instance when it comes to money, the more responsible with your giving that you are. the more you are likely to receive money in return. A hand that is closed tightly around money ensures nothing leaves, but also ensures no more can come in. An open hand allows more to come in and leave freely.

CART RETURNERS ARE DISCIPLINED

At some point, whether you are stressed out because of a young child screaming, or a frazzled parent trying to make it home in time for dinner after running late from work. We have all been tempted to turn to the dark side, right? Your child is screaming, and the nearest cart receptacle is like seven parking spaces away. "Can't I leave the cart here just this once?"

These are the moments that define us. Will you stand strong or break to temptation? Look on the bright side; that screaming child ensures that everyone will look and see you doing the right thing.

Walking the seven spaces also shows you are disciplined. You have committed yourself to a moral standard that you will not break. Discipline is an attractive quality in people. Employers look for it in their employees and people look for it in their potential spouses. They want to know they can trust you to do the right thing no matter what the circumstances.

Disciplined people tend to be more successful with money as well. Sticking to a budget and saving money is not easy. There always seems to be budget busting purchases we can justify. If we do not have the self-control to resist deserting our shopping cart, will we have the self-control to turn away from an impulsive purchase?

CART RETURNERS ARE HAPPIER PEOPLE

I know I have addressed it already, but I will say it again. Cart returning shows you are not selfish. Which is good because selfish people are not happy.

Giving to others brings happiness into our lives. Whether it is a big or small gesture, they can make a lasting impact. Focusing only on ourselves gives us a negative outlook on life and will not bring us the long-term desires we are hoping for. We tend to only think about the things we do not have, the things we want, or the things others have that we wish we had. None of these bring on a spirit of gratitude or contentment.

By finding a way to give to others it will change your outlook. Giving takes the focus off yourself and puts it on others. This can even benefit your budget. When you are not focused on yourself, you tend to spend less money on yourself. Funny how that works out.

At the end of the day, the only person you can control is you. As infuriating as it is to see a front row parking space blocked by a deserted cart, take comfort in knowing that you still have the upper hand.

To all my cart deserters out there, it is never too late to make a change. Cart returners are very forgiving and will welcome you to our side with open arms.

Finally, to all my cart returners, while the walk to the receptacle may be treacherous, the walk back to your car can be empowering. You did the right thing. Hold your head up high, pump your fist in the air, and consider that walk as your victory lap.

At the end of the day, you must return the shopping cart out of the goodness of your own heart. You must return the shopping cart because it is the right thing to do. Because it is correct.

CHAPTER 1

KNOW THE WHY

"When your why is big enough, you will find your how." –
Les Brown

What do Martin Luther King, Jr., Steve Jobs, and the Wright brothers have in common? On the face of it, not a lot. They worked on different projects for different reasons at different times. But there is one thing that unites the four of them: they all understood that no one buys into an idea, project, or product unless they understand why it exists. That fact is something you will find in every great leader and successful organization. Think of it as a sense of purpose. People do their best work and inspire others when they know why they are doing what they are doing. This does not mean striving to make money. It means engaging in purposeful activity, an approach that often results in financial gain.

SUCCESS IS THE FRUIT OF DESIGN, NOT SHORT-TERM PATCHES

When two organizations view the inside of each of their operations, they tend to look the same. But when you look deeper, that is where you generally will find several nuances that distinguishes one organization from another. While one organization may look to get the job done, the other tends to focus on not only getting the job done, but also getting the job done right. Instead of looking at a problem and attempting to figure out a quick, makeshift solution, you should take time from the outset to engineer the outcome you want from the beginning that is always the best way to go.

The unfortunate reality is that in life and in business, things do not generally work in a lean, mean, and efficient way. Faced with a result that does not match up with an original plan, leaders often turn to perfectly effective short-term patches to achieve their goals. This might keep things chugging along in the interim, but it is not the best approach.

Those that are successful build products and provide services according to a blueprint, they make things fit by design, not by default. Every instruction a leader gives, every course of action they put in motion, and every target they set begins with the same thing, a decision. Some decide to put the square peg in the round hole; others start somewhere very different.

Manipulating people brings short-term benefits but undermines long-term viability. The reality is that manipulation comes in different forms. In general, it is anything that pushes someone to buy, think clearance sales, two-for-one deals, advertising hype, or appeals to authority in claims like "Four out of five dentists prefer Trident." It is a popular strategy and in the short term, at least, it is effective. Unfortunately, it rarely pays in the long run. Take one of the most common forms of manipulation, the "price game." Drop your prices low enough and folks will buy your products. This is catnip to sellers. There is a fantastic short-term gain, but it quickly becomes a habit that is hard to kick. The lower your prices, the more reluctant your customers will be to pay more. The result: slimmer margins that can only be offset by more sales, which in turn require even lower prices.

Even companies that maintain profitability while sinking their prices tend to suffer. Walmart, for example, has a healthy bottom line. Its reputation, however, is and has been in tatters. The only way of making money while offering consumers constant bargains is to cut costs elsewhere. Today, Walmart is notorious for its shoddy treatment of underpaid and overworked employees in its in US stores. Worse, manipulation might be able to drive transactions and individual sales, but it does not breed loyalty.

You can see why when you think of how rewards work. When you lose your kitten and offer a reward to whoever returns it to you, for example, you are not trying to build a relationship with the finder, you just want your cat back. That is not a sustainable basis for a business.

AFFIRM BELIEFS AND VALUES

Companies like Apple do not just sell products, they affirm their customers' beliefs and values. When you get down to it, Apple is just another computer company. Like Dell, HP, or Toshiba, Apple has some systems that work well and some that do not. All four firms have equal access to resources, talent, and media channels to publicize their products. Rationally speaking, it does not matter which company's product you choose, and they are all decent. But that is not how it works. In the real world, folks pay a lot more for Apple devices and stand in line for hours for the latest iPhone.

The reason is that Apple is different. Unlike its rivals, it is not associated with a single product category. This is unusual in today's economy and community. Typically, you would expect customers to buy their computers from one company, their cell phones from another, and their mp3 players from a third. Apple has been hugely successful in all three market categories. There is a good reason for this: the why matters more than the what.

Let us break that down. Most organizations have a straightforward pitch. They describe what they do, state why they are better than their competitors, and wrap things up with a call to action. If Apple were like most other companies, its pitch would be simple: "We make great computers, they're beautifully designed and user-friendly, wanna buy one?"

But that's not what Apple says. Here's its actual message, the pitch that has made it one of the most successful companies of all time: "Everything we do is about challenging the status quo. We believe in thinking differently, and we prove this by making beautiful, user-friendly products. Oh, and we also happen to make great computers. Wanna buy one?" Notice the difference? There is no manipulation or free stuff. In fact, the emphasis is not really on products at all. Apple is not telling us what it makes, it is telling us why it does what it does.

This is a great example of beginning with why. Apple is not arguing that we should buy a Mac or an iPhone Pro Max because they are better and cheaper than rival devices, or because they have been endorsed by Kendall Jenner. It is telling us that if we also believe in creativity and thinking outside the box, Apple is the right company for us. Put differently, it "gets us" and it sees us as people with beliefs and values rather than as mere consumers.

OUR RATIONAL BRAIN DOES NOT CONTROL OUR DECISIONS

Here is a tricky question: Why do you love your spouse? Often, we will say something like, "Well, I don't know, she's funny and smart." But there are millions, even billions of funny and smart people out there with whom we do not want to share our lives. Or we might say, "He completes me." But how on Earth do you look for someone who does that? These are not the real reasons we fall in love, they are attempts to describe something that is virtually indescribable. There is a reason for that.

If you look at a cross-section of the human brain, you will see three areas. Do not worry, we are only going to review this from a high-level once so you will not need to be a brain surgeon to grasp this concept. On the outside is the most recently evolved part, it is called the neocortex. This is responsible for rational thought and language. The two middle sections make up what is called the limbic brain. These are responsible for feelings like loyalty and trust, as well as decision-making.

Crucially, these older areas lack the capacity for language. That is why it is so hard to describe why you love someone. It also explains why companies fail to connect with customers. Say you are trying to sell a TV. You explain its price, specs, and features. All this data is a great way of engaging the neocortex, but here is the rub: People can process vast amounts of complex information, but information is not what drives behavior. If you want to change behavior, you need to access the limbic brain. Take an example from the laundry-detergent industry.

For years, American companies made commercials claiming that their detergents made people's whites whiter and their brights brighter. On the face of it, this was a solid value proposition that, after all, was what market research had shown consumers wanted from their detergent. Because researchers had asked consumers what they wanted, they spent all their time talking about how their product worked. Some claimed protein was the miracle ingredient; others pointed to their patented color enhancers. But that is not why we clean our clothes.

We assume that all detergents get our clothes clean and that is just what they do. Studies continue to find that when we take our clothes out of the machine, we do not hold them up to the light to inspect how white or bright they are. We smell them. Feeling clean matters more than objective cleanliness. The whole detergent industry was acting on a false assumption. That just goes to show why it is worth starting with why.

THE LAW OF DIFFUSION

Innovations spread far and wide when they are championed by a minority of true believers. Can you imagine spending $15,000 on a new type of TV that could be the next big thing but might just be a flop? No? You are not alone. Only a small minority embraces new products and ideas, but this sliver of the consumer population is vital to the success of companies and organizations looking to reach a mass audience. This is called the law of diffusion, a concept that goes back to a 1962 book by communications theorist Everett M. Rogers. His theory states that every population can be divided into five segments, each of which responds differently to innovation.

Innovators, who make up 2.5 percent of the population, are the first to embrace novelty. The next 13.5 percent are early adopters. Then come the more risk-averse early majority and the late majority. Together, they account for 68 percent of the population. The final 16 percent are laggards folks who only buy touch-tone phones because rotary phones do not exist anymore.

Innovators and early adopters are happy to pay a premium or suffer inconveniences to own a product or espouse an idea because it feels right. This has little to do with the true merits of that product or idea and a lot to do with their own sense of themselves. Most people do not make these kinds of intuitive decisions, however. They do not want a phone or TV that aligns with their values; they want something that works and does not cost too much.

The irony of mass-market success is that it is impossible to achieve if you are trying to convince the practical-minded majority. The reason is the majority will not try something until someone else has recommended it to them. If you want to reach the middle of community, you need a minority of loyalists to get the word out, something they will only do if they believe in your why.

This is not true only in business. In August 1963, 250,000 people stood in the scorching sun in Washington, DC, to hear Martin Luther King, Jr. talk. No invitations had been sent out and there was not a website to check, but word had spread. Dr. King was not the only man who had suffered in pre-civil rights America or the only great orator in the nation, but he never stopped talking about what he believed and why he believed it. His message had been taken up by a small following who had made it their own. By 1963, it had finally reached middle America.

YOU RUN INTO TROUBLE WHEN YOU LOSE YOUR SENSE OF "WHY"

Imagine a small mid-century retail establishment in the United States. The company's founder came of age during the Great Depression and believes in hard work and fairness. Look after folks, he likes to say, and they will take care of you. The business gradually grows, but it never loses sight of its founding ideals. Sure, prices are low, but that is not what makes the company so popular. What people really love is its holistic philosophy of giving back to employees, customers, and the community.

This is the company we just talked about, but you might not have heard it described in this way. It is Walmart. So, what went wrong? Walmart's original values did not outlive its founder, Sam Walton. After his death in 1992, the retail giant lost its way. Abandoning its earlier commitment to the communities in which it operated, it redefined its mission as selling more and more at the lowest possible price. This new orientation was not down to external competition and in fact, Walmart was in better shape than ever. All in all, Walmart was racking up more year sales year over year and exceeding internal and external expectations.

This should have been a golden age for Walmart, but that is not how it felt inside the corporation. This is an unfortunate, common, yet avoidable problem with a lot of companies these days. Like the leaders of other larger corporations for the most part, they had lost its sense of purpose, the why. A little over a decade ago, it was facing almost a hundred new class-action lawsuits for violating its employees' rights and had already paid out millions of dollars to settle previous cases. Towns and cities that would have once welcomed the opening of new Walmart stores now fought tooth and nail to keep the company out of their communities.

Another example can be seen in our country's mission to flight and when those who focus on the "what" often fail, while those that begin with "why" are capable of extraordinary achievements. Over a century ago, Samuel Pierpont Langley had it all figured out: he was going to be the first man to fly. He was a well-connected senior officer at the Smithsonian Institute, he had friends in high places, people like Andrew Carnegie and Alexander Graham Bell and his contacts had helped him land a $50,000 research grant from the US War Department. He was able to assemble the brightest minds in the United States to help him become the first to flight.

Reporters from the New York Times followed him all around, and the public was rooting for him. His success was virtually guaranteed. But despite his hard work and numerous attempts, he just could not get his contraption off the ground. Here is why.

It was on December 17, 1903, a small group of onlookers witnessed a man, not Langley take flight for the first time in human history in the "flying machine", he had built by two brothers several years prior, Wilbur and Orville Wright, and their team. No one involved held a college degree, and the project had been funded by proceeds from the Wrights' bicycle shop. How in the world did they achieve what Langley could not? They began with why.

Wilbur and Orville were true scientists who cared deeply and genuinely about the problem they were trying to solve, which was the problem of flight and balance. More importantly, they knew that if they succeeded, it would change the world forever. Langley, by contrast, was obsessed with the what. He wanted the fame and prestige that came with a major scientific breakthrough and was indifferent to its application. When the Wrights beat him to it, he did not attempt to improve on their flying machine, he simply gave up. Orville and Wilbur also had another string to their bow: a dedicated team. By practicing what they preached, they inspired others to join them. Every day, this motley crew of dreamers and tinkerers returned to the field behind the Wrights' shop with five sets of parts. After five failures, they trudged in and ate dinner. The next day, they started again.

Both Langley and the Wright brothers were highly motivated and had a strong work ethic and keen scientific minds. Langley, however, had paid for talent to help him make his name. The Wrights' commitment to altering the course of history excited those around them and filled them with belief. And that is the lesson here. Hire people for what they can do for you and they will work for your money. Hire people who believe in your why, on the other hand, and they will give you their blood, sweat, and tears.

NOTES:

CHAPTER 2

TWO EARS, ONE MOUTH

"Seek first to understand, then to be understood." –
Stephen Covey

In nearly every kind of relationship and across all professions, we come into situations where we need to motivate people to do something, act a certain way or even just get them to listen to us. Unfortunately, despite how often we are in these situations, we are generally not very good at persuading people to do what we want. What we want is for people to "buy in," i.e., become invested in us and thus be open to what we have to say. However, because we are often too caught up in ourselves and our own problems, we lose the ability to communicate well and effectively shoot ourselves in the foot. To accomplish this, you must stop talking and start listening.

LISTENING IS A KEY TO OVERCOMING RESISTANCE AND INITIATING PROGRESS

Have you ever stopped to consider the rhythm of your everyday conversations? If so, you might have found that you approach them as if they were all rational arguments, and this can often be counterproductive. In fact, using arguments or pressure to influence or convince others often creates resistance. This is especially true when people come to you in times of stress: they do not want advice to improve their situation, they just want to share what is going on with them.

Listening gives others the chance to share their feelings and concerns, which creates a space for taking the next steps and making arguments. When we feel like our concerns are being heard, it gives concern to a certain level of trust between us and our conversation partners. If you want people to be open to your arguments, you must listen first. And, as you will discover in this chapter, we are biologically programmed to do just that.

When our emotions are mirrored back to us, we feel positive emotions. Surely, you have heard the adage "Monkey see, monkey do," right? As it turns out, it is true. Indeed, we are constantly mirroring those around us, i.e., recognizing, acknowledging, and reciprocating the feelings and emotions of the individuals we are engaged with. Interestingly, mirroring is programmed into our brains: brain cells called mirror neurons allow us to experience what we perceive that others are feeling. Mirror neurons are called "monkey see, monkey do" neurons for good reason: if you've ever cringed when you saw a friend or co-worker get a paper cut and almost feeling the pain yourself or started to tear up when you saw someone else cry, then you've experienced your mirror neurons in action.

Some scientists believe these neurons could even be the basis for human empathy. In fact, researchers have called mirror neurons "empathy neurons" because of the way they bring people closer together. These are also what cause us to constantly try to appease those around us, satisfy others' wishes and expectations, and seek their approval. For example, when a speaker notices that their audience has become unresponsive, constantly looking at their watches or staring off into space, these are what cause them to respond to their desires by saying: "Okay, it's time for a break."

However, when our feelings are not met with empathy, but instead with apathy, hostility, or other negative responses, we are less likely to feel connected to others. Studies continue to show that if we mirror others but are not mirrored in return, we develop a deficit in our own mirror receptors. When these deficits occur, we feel alone and disconnected. Whether it is because we engage in so much impersonal communication via email or mobile phones or because we have less time to form connections, we no longer mirror each other the way we used to.

LISTENING RELIES ON THE RATIONAL, NOT THE EMOTIONAL OR INSTINCTUAL PART OF OUR BRAINS

Have you ever felt like you were having an argument with yourself? Like your consciousness was divided into different "yous"? Well, your brain really is divided into three different thinking parts, or layers, and they all experience and react to the world differently. Our reptilian layer is very primitive and is all about reacting to the immediate situation. This layer is responsible for our fight-or-flight reactions. It does not take the time to ponder or analyze situations: it acts. Or: it does not. Sometimes the reptilian layer causes a deer-in-the-headlights reaction, i.e., we freeze up and cannot act at all.

The next layer, the mammalian layer, is a bit more evolved than the reptilian layer: it oversees our emotions and is the home of your inner drama queen. The mammalian layer is where powerful feelings arise, including emotions like anger, jealousy, love, grief, pleasure, joy, and sadness.

Lastly, there is the rational, reasoning layer. This layer of the brain is responsible for collecting and analyzing the data from the reptilian and mammalian layers of the brain and developing logical next steps. Just how you have different thinking layers that influence how you react to the world, so do your conversation partners. If you want them to be receptive to what you have to say, you will have to make sure that they are thinking with the right layer. Let us dive into just how to make sure your conversation partners have the right mindset to communicate effectively.

One thing you can do is make sure that you and your conversation partner are using your rational brains. If you want to be able to listen to and reach others, you must get your own emotions under control first. Emotions like fear, anger or panic will hinder your ability to reason and develop nuanced strategies. Unfortunately, we will not always be able to stay in control. Luckily, when we lose our cool, we can regain control over and access to the rational layer by simply acknowledging threats or panic.

When it comes to threatening situations, the brain's reasoning layer shuts down and passes control over to the emotional side of the brain. Feeling threatened can also trigger the fight-or-flight mechanisms that cause logical reasoning to freeze and allow your immediate emotions and instincts to take over. However, by expressing your feelings of fear or panic aloud, you give yourself the opportunity to calm down and look for solutions.

In fact, studies have shown that simply naming threats and fears cools down that part of the brain, causing our reptilian brain to cede control, passing it back to our rational brain. Knowing this, you should also give others the space they need to address their fears when things start getting out of control. This way, they can listen to your arguments again with a clear and rational mind.

SHOWING VULNERABILITY IS EMPOWERING AND GIVES OTHERS THE CHANCE TO LISTEN TO US

One of the most difficult parts of becoming a good communicator is accepting your vulnerability. However, your vulnerability is a tool: when you show vulnerable emotions, like helplessness or fear, you give others the chance to connect and respond. As we have seen, mirroring is a critical part of identifying with others. However, others can only mirror what you show them, so if you hide your emotions, you will not be truly understood.

Imagine you are nervous about a big presentation, but you also feel ashamed of being so nervous. Your colleague makes an insensitive remark to you and you respond with anger. Because you are showing anger, you are more likely to get anger in return. However, if you had instead shown your genuine emotions, i.e., your nervousness, your colleague probably would have been able to empathize with you and boost your confidence before the meeting. Furthermore, giving others the opportunity to show their vulnerability enables you both to explore what is behind the emotions.

The reality is, when you level with others they will be more relaxed and open for dialogue. If there is one thing we all love talking about, it's ourselves. And you can use this to your advantage when you want people to be open and become invested in your interaction. Using questions to establish an atmosphere of equality with your conversation partner will create a stronger connection. One way to do this is with the Side-by-Side approach, in which you ask questions during a shared moment and then follow up with more questions to deepen the connection.

Demonstrating real interest in others will make them feel valuable, and thus bring the dialogue to a deeper level. The best way to make others feel understood and valued is through empathy. Although we know how powerful empathy can be, showing empathy is not always intuitive.

Here is a script you can follow that will guide you towards empathy:

First, attach an emotion to what the person you are talking to is feeling. Let us use anger as an example.

Next, ask them if your perceptions are accurate by saying something like: *"I'm trying to get a sense of what you're feeling, and I think it's anger. Is that correct? If not, what are you feeling?"*

Then, once you have established which emotion they are feeling, ask: *"How angry are you?"* Be prepared for an emotional response and allow plenty of time for their answer. Remember: this is not about you, so do not get defensive.

Next, find out why they are angry by saying something like: *"And the reason you're so angry is because ...?"*

After they have answered, say: *"Tell me, what needs to happen for that anger to subside?"*

Finally, find out how the two of you can work together to move forward; ask: *"What can I do to make that happen? What can you do to make that happen?"*

By demonstrating empathy, they will feel "felt," thus allowing you both to connect and move forward together.

.

.

NOTES:

CHAPTER 3

MASTER THE FIELD OF SELF-AWARENESS

"What is necessary to change a person is to change his awareness of himself." – Abraham Maslow

FOR LASTING CHANGE, YOU MUST ADDRESS YOUR CHARACTER, NOT JUST YOUR BEHAVIOR

There are two ways to strive for improvements to your life:

1. The first method is to work on the skills necessary for the behavior you desire. We can call this method the personality ethic. The personality ethic lets you avoid working on the fundamental character traits that are holding you back, promising that some easily learnable technique will be the silver bullet for all your problems. Unfortunately, this promise is usually empty, and it almost never results in lasting personal growth.

2. The second method is far more effective: working on your character, that is, the fundamental habits and belief systems that form your view of the world. Only behavior stemming straight from your character will endure over time, because, sooner or later, your true character will shine through. This can be called the character ethic, and it emphasizes things like courage, integrity, and the golden rule.

So, if you really want to change, you need to work from the inside out. That is why it is important to align your way of seeing the world with basic universal principles. If you have ever tried to navigate the streets of a foreign city, you know that a map is useful. But when you navigate the world around you, instead of a map with streets and addresses, you use your standards to guide you. A standard is the subjective way each of us perceives and understands the world. After all, no one is really an objective observer. Everything we understand about the world is tinted by our own standards.

Since our standards are at the core of our characters, shifting them is the key to making lasting changes. Only in this way can we change our subjective realities and, with them, our characters, and behaviors. Therefore, you need to recognize and monitor your own standards; if you do not, you will not know which ones are holding you back. So which standards should you strive for?

The most effective are the ones aligned with larger, universal principles, like fairness, honesty, and integrity. Since most people agree that these principles are good, we can see them as permanent, natural laws. Therefore, the more accurately your map of standards reflects this landscape of natural principles, the more realistic your view and the better your chances of success in attaining lasting change. Attaining this kind of principle-based standard is exactly what appropriate self-awareness habits are all about.

I highly recommend that you focus on being proactive instead of reactive and do your best to take control of your own fate. Because what distinguishes humans from animals is that animals are inferior to external stimuli and can only react to these stimuli in the preprogrammed way that is in their nature. We humans, in contrast, can reflect on a stimuli before responding to it, and we can even reprogram ourselves to respond in a specific, desirable way. This means that instead of just reacting to the world around us, we can proactively influence it.

But even though we all have this capacity for proactivity, many people still choose to be reactive and allow external circumstances to dictate their behavior and emotions. You can hear it in the way such people speak; phrases like "It wasn't my fault", "It's out of my hands", or the one I dislike the most "it is what it is" are extremely common. People who are proactive, on the other hand, make their own weather. They assume responsibility for their own lives and make conscious choices about their behavior. They say things like "I've decided to..." or "Let us try to find a solution to this problem."

Another way to understand the difference between the two attitudes is to imagine two aligned circles. The outer circle is your Circle of Concern, representing all the things you are concerned about, ranging from the water bill to the threat of a global pandemic. Inside this circle is the smaller Circle of Influence, which represents all the things you can do something about. Proactive people focus on their Circles of Influence, choosing to work on the things within their control. And this results in the expansion of their Circles of Influence. Meanwhile, reactive people focus on their Circles of Concern, fretting over things they cannot alter. This results in their Circle of Influence shrinking.

Proactivity can be a profoundly powerful habit. It even works in the most extreme circumstances. You have the power to decide what happens in the gap between a stimulus and your response. Thus, you can change your behavior and your emotions. To put this into practice, commit to a thirty-day proactivity challenge: Whether at home or at work, whenever you catch yourself blaming someone or something external for a problem you face, remind yourself that the root cause is your reaction to the problem. Focus on finding solutions instead of accusing others. Exercise the tiny freedom you have before you respond, and you will find your capacity for proactivity flourishing.

VISUALIZE THE ENDING BEFORE YOU EVEN START

Whenever you perform an action, you are performing it twice: first in your mind, when you imagine it, and then physically, when you do it. Therefore, it is crucial to have the desired end firmly in your mind before you start any task. The more exact and realistic the mental picture of the action is, the better its execution will be and, hence, the better the results. This kind of visual anticipation works in all possible situations.

So, whether at work or at home, take the time required for visualization. As the saying goes, "Better to ask twice than to lose your way once." It is much more productive to spend time anticipating an action and visualizing the desired outcome than just plowing hastily on, possibly in the wrong direction. To get started, you could think about one of your upcoming projects and write down exactly what results you desire and what steps you will take to attain those results. But visualizing the ending before you even start is not just important for individual projects. You should also have a clear view of your larger life goals.

One thing I decided to do many years ago was to sit down and write a personal mission statement and integrate it into my daily life. Even though it is a small mental exercise, it has very large benefits. Start by imagining that it is five years in the future, and, sadly enough, you have died. Take a moment to visualize your own funeral. Imagine your loved ones, your spouse, your best friend, maybe your dearest co-worker, giving eulogies. Now ask yourself what you would like them to say. What sort of person do you want to be remembered as? For what do you want to be remembered?

Unfortunately, many people spend their time working toward goals that do not really matter to them, because they never stopped to define them properly. In short, they fail to understand the difference between being efficient and being effective. Being efficient means getting the maximum amount done in the shortest amount of time. But this is pointless if you do not know what you are striving for and why you are doing it. It is a bit like climbing a ladder that is set against the wrong wall: you are making progress, but in the wrong direction.

Being effective, on the other hand, means having your ladder on the right wall and you know what your destination in life is. Effective people do not just thoughtlessly pursue things like money and fame; they focus on what is important to them. Everything else is a waste. You can clarify your destination by asking yourself those funeral questions, and then use your answers as a basis for writing a personal mission statement. This is a document where you define your own creed, meaning what kind of person you want to be, what you hope to achieve in your life, as well as the basic values and principles underlying these goals.

The mission statement should become your personal constitution, an established standard by which everything else can be measured and valued. Having such a compass gives you a sense of direction and security, and it enables you to at least try to align all your actions with it. Some thoughts that could be included in a person's mission statement might be "I value my work, but my family comes first and I will seek to balance my time spent on them. I value a just and fair community and will strive to make my voice heard in political decisions. I will be proactive in pursuing my life goals and will not simply be swept along by circumstances." And so on.

ACTION EXPRESSES PRIORITIES

Now that you have a mission statement, you must proactively take charge and make it into a reality by living it, day in and day out. Of course, during your everyday hassles, roles, and relationships, this can be challenging, and it demands good time-management skills.

Unfortunately, most time-management techniques focus on increasing efficiency, not on improving effectiveness. But the good news is that you do not really need complicated techniques. Most of the time it is good enough to remember: "action expresses priorities".

This means rigorously prioritizing everything you do so that the important things are always taken care of first, while everything else is put aside and then dealt with or delegated later. Focus on the actions that will have an enormously positive impact on your life. And when you work enough in this area, you will find far fewer crises emerging in less important areas. Unfortunately, many people do not understand the importance of tasks that are important but not urgent. A good first step in implementing this habit in your life is to identify an important-urgent activity that you've been neglecting, one that would have a significant impact on your life if you did it well and then commit in writing to doing more of it.

In today's competitive world it all tends to center around winning. But when you interact with others, it is important to not focus on a "must win" attitude outcome. You see, most people's worldviews are shaped by a strong "win-lose" paradigm. This means they see any interaction with others, whether at work or in their personal life, as basically a competition, where they need to fight the other person for the bigger slice of pie. But most situations in life do not need to be competitions. There is usually enough pie for everyone, and it is far better when all parties work toward a "win-win" solution that is beneficial for everyone, rather than fighting for a "win-lose" outcome.

A major disadvantage of the "win-lose" mentality is when two people of this mentality come up against each other, the situation usually becomes a "lose-lose" one. After a bitter fight, both parties end up losing. But if you think" win-win," you will find yourself building lots of positive relationships because each interaction strengthens the relationship, rather than eroding it.

You need to form stable relationships with others, and this means investing in emotional bank accounts. A relationship with another person is kind of like a bank account, albeit an emotional one: by putting time, effort and good will into it, the balance of the account grows, reflecting the increasing trust between the two parties. A healthy balance on your account means that both parties are flexible, and any miscommunications are quickly sorted out. If, on the other hand, the balance is zero, there is no flexibility and the relationship is like a battlefield: every word must be carefully chosen to avoid explosive conflict.

The way that you can grow your account balance in an emotional bank account could be by finding a win-win solution, sticking to promises you two have made, or really listening empathically to another person. A withdrawal, on the other hand, would be fighting for a win-lose solution, breaking a promise, or only halfheartedly listening to the other person. To build strong, long-lasting relationships, there are several major deposits you can make: always keep promises, be explicit about what you expect of the other person and be courteous and sensitive even in small matters.

Another major deposit is maintaining the utmost personal integrity. This means being loyal to those who are not present, and never bad-mouthing them or revealing what they have told you in confidence. This will prove to those who are present that you can be trusted. But perhaps one of the most important deposits you can make is really trying to understand other people, because this deposit allows you to discover what is important to them and thus which things, they consider deposits.

DO NOT JUST LISTEN TO REPLY, LISTEN TO APPLY

In everyday life, when talking to others we often do not really listen to what the other person has to say and instead project our own situation onto them, coming up with quick solutions that we can "prescribe" to them. In general, such advice is seldom welcome, since people usually only trust someone's judgment if they feel their situations have been fully understood. So, if you want to be respected as a listener and an imparter of advice, you need to develop the skill of empathic listening. This necessitates a change of "I'm listening so that I can provide an answer" to "I'm listening so that I can really understand the person in front of me."

Empathic listening means trying to get inside the other person's frame of reference so you can understand them both intellectually and emotionally. According to experts in communication, the words we say account for just ten percent of our communication, while the sounds account for thirty percent and our body language for sixty percent. So, to practice empathic listening, you should not just listen to the words; you should attend to the feeling, behavior and meaning behind them. One way to work on your empathic listening skills is to observe a conversation without hearing the words.

When you do that, what emotions do you see being communicated? It takes time and effort to master this skill, but the later rewards are well worth it. If you learn to listen in a truly empathic way, you will notice that many people are fully prepared to open to you and let them know what is going on with them in that moment so you may be able to help and to reciprocate by considering your opinions and advice. They just need a good, appreciative listener before they can do so.

Synergy means a situation where the contributions of many add up to a total that exceeds the combined contributions of the individuals. To synergize is to treat others with openness and respect. One plus one can equal three or more on some occasions, meaning that the contributions of a few working together in unison can equate to extra efforts of additional help. You can implement this principle in your own social interactions by seeing the world differently and understanding we each have our own strengths. Leverage the power of synergy by being open with others and valuing these differences.

When people truly synergize, they listen to each other, put themselves in each other's shoes and use the contributions of others as a springboard to create something great. They are on the same side, trying to tackle a shared challenge, not fighting each other. The path to synergizing starts with seeing your interactions with others as an adventure. The outcome of that adventure may not be completely under your control, but you should still embrace it with complete openness. This requires a significant degree of self-confidence, as well as the conviction that the combined contribution of each party can lead to something great, even if the journey to get there is a bit chaotic.

PRESERVE AND ENHANCE YOUR GREATEST ASSET

If you never pause to take care of yourself, any gains in effectiveness you achieve will be short-lived, for you will soon exhaust yourself and won't be able to maintain any of the good habits you've developed. That is why making sure you preserve and enhance your greatest asset is essential for lasting effectiveness in every area of your physical and mental parts of your life.

To stay in good shape, you need to exercise regularly, eat healthy, and avoid undue stress. Your spiritual health also contributes to lasting effectiveness. This could mean praying or meditating, or simply regularly reflecting on your own norms and values. To stay mentally healthy, read plenty of good books, avoid spending too much time in front of your television screen and make time for your own writing in some form. Organizing and planning things are also good exercises to keep your mind sharp and fresh. Finally, it is important to take care of your social and emotional health by deliberately seeking to understand others, building positive relationships with them, and working on projects that help improve their lives.

Consciously make time to recuperate and recharge. Many people claim they cannot find time for this, but in the long-term, it is essential for sustained effectiveness and the rewards in productivity and well-being that come with it. To make sure you truly preserve and enhance your greatest asset, write down activities that could contribute to your well-being in every area of your physical and mental parts of your life. Then pick one activity as a goal for the week and, afterwards, evaluate your performance. This will help you strive for balanced renewal in all areas.

NOTES:

CHAPTER 4

COMMUNICATION

"Effective communication is about what you say, how you say it, and when you say it." – Nick Jarman

Do you sometimes struggle to make friends or argue with others and still do not manage to win them over to your way of thinking? Do you feel like your relationships with your colleagues and clients could be better? Then this chapter is for you as we talk about how you can overcome these woes quickly. When these techniques are put into use, you will become a more likeable, persuasive, and effective person, professional and leader.

DO NOT CRITICIZE OTHERS IF YOU WANT THEM TO LIKE YOU

When something goes wrong or does not go the way you plan, should you yell at them? Scold them? Criticize them? No, because kindness was something that psychologists had discovered a long time ago: they found when even animals were rewarded for good behavior, they learned more effectively than those punished for bad behavior. The same is true of people: criticizing them will not encourage them to change their behavior because they are not primarily driven by reason but by emotion. Thus, the person you criticize will not truly listen to what you are saying. They will just feel like they are under attack, and their natural reaction will be to dig in and fight back.

So, while voicing criticism might help you blow off steam, in the long-term, it will just make others like you less. Many successful people make it a habit to never openly criticize others, they do not criticize others at all actually; they have found this technique to be very successful under even the most stressful circumstances. Criticizing someone is easy, but it takes character to be understanding and to forgive others for their mistakes and shortcomings. So, if you want others to like you, think about why they did what they did, accept their shortcomings and make it a rule to never criticize them openly.

When you show your appreciation frequently and make them feel important, they will in turn return the favors to you. One of the strongest drivers of human behavior is the desire to be appreciated by others; we all like being complimented and hearing that we are doing a good job. Some people even claim that all of civilization ultimately rests upon the human desire to be important. Our craving for approval and praise makes us climb the highest mountains, buy a sports team, and found multi-billion-dollar companies.

No one is immune to this longing for importance and appreciation. But you do not need to give someone a fancy title to show your appreciation. It is enough to use simple phrases like "Thank you" and "I'm sorry," while also giving sincere, honest praise. Do not shower people with phony flattery though, or they will see right through it. Instead, stop thinking about yourself for a moment and focus on the good points of the person in front of you.

Also, be sure to make the other person feel important. To get into the right mind-set, try thinking that every person you meet was superior to you in certain ways, so there was always something to learn from and appreciate in other people. Or think about the Golden Rule: treat others as you would like others to treat you. The next time you see a tired, bored, underappreciated service employee somewhere, try to brighten their day with some appreciation. Leave little sparks of appreciation in your wake and you will be surprised to see how positively people react when their hunger for recognition is fed.

You will soon become someone whom others like and enjoy working with. And best of all, you will have a positive impact on the lives of those around you.

HERE IS ONE WAY TO MAKE A GOOD FIRST IMPRESSION, SMILE

If someone we have just met smiles at us, we tend to automatically like them from the onset. The smile of a baby, for instance, immediately makes us feel warm and fuzzy inside, as does seeing a dog wagging its tail out of sheer delight at seeing us. So, if you want to make yourself instantly likeable to someone, show them that you are happy to see them by smiling. When they see how happy you are to meet them, they cannot help but be happy to see you too.

And as if this wasn't a big enough benefit on its own, psychologists have also uncovered a positive side-effect of smiling: it seems that the connection between positive emotions and smiling is not a one-way street; consciously smiling can lead to positive emotions, just as positive emotions can lead to smiling. In other words, even though a smile costs nothing, you can use it to lift your spirits and those of others. If you would like to smile more but do not feel like it, just try forcing yourself: whistle, sing or hum a tune. Act as if you are already cheerful and you will soon find yourself becoming happier.

Something else that makes each of us uniquely happy is related to the sweetest sound we know, our name. So, to win someone's favor be sure to remember their name and use it in conversation frequently. Be sure you catch the name when it comes up the first time in conversation and ask for it to be repeated or even spelled out if needed. Then repeat it back to the person multiple times to associate it with the person to whom you are talking. Finally, when you are alone, write it down to enforce the memory. And you need not stop at remembering the other person' name. Make it a habit of finding out the birthdays of people you meet so that you can send them a card, text, or email wishing them a happy birthday. You can imagine how appreciated they will feel, especially when often you are the only one who remembered.

I remember one of the first times my family and I sat down at a restaurant with our favorite family Blue and Dorothy' Adams. There were about seven or eight of us at the table, half were kids and the waitress came over and took our orders. After the waitress walked away Dorothy put a twenty-dollar bill on the table and said whoever remembers her name gets the money. My daughter Isabella who had never played this game before remembered the waitress's name and won the twenty bucks. Ever since that meal over fifteen years ago, my wife Joani incorporates this into every dinner my family and I go out to.

IF YOU WANT TO BE INTERESTING YOURSELF, BE A GOOD LISTENER

It turns out that the secret of being interesting yourself is simply to be interested in others. As we learned a lot about in Chapter 2, we all love a good listener, especially when they encourage us to speak about ourselves. That is because humans are always interested in talking about themselves, which is why we are always overjoyed to meet someone who shares this interest. So, if you want to be more likeable and interesting, stop talking and just listen. Ask others about themselves and encourage them to speak at length.

When conversing, most people get so preoccupied with what they want to say next that they barely listen to the other person at all. Truly listening means making a conscious effort to give the other person your full attention. And the benefits of this approach are substantial. On the other hand, talking about yourself a lot, failing to listen to others and constantly interrupting them will make you instantly dislikeable because these traits signal that you are self-centered. So, give listening a try.

A lot of times it works well when you think about what others want and talk about what is important to them. Do you like chocolate? Probably. But if you were to go fishing, would you bait your hook with it? Of course not, because in fishing it does not matter what you want. What matters is what the fish want. Similarly, if you want someone else to do something, you are better off thinking about it from their perspective: how you can make them want to do it?

A crucial piece of advice to win someone's favor is to become knowledgeable and speak about things that are important to them. People become very fond of those who speak about things they are interested in themselves, such as their jobs, hobbies or million-dollar checks. Or try this, whenever you are about to meet a new person, prepare for the meeting by reading everything you can about the other person's interests. Try to understand that the route to someone's good graces is talking about the things they value the most. And if you are not sure about the other person's interests, remember that there is one topic everyone is interested in: themselves. Talk to people about themselves, and they will listen for hours.

Another piece of advice is to avoid all arguments because they cannot be won. You see, arguing with another person does not really make much sense. If you lose, you lose the argument. If you win, the other person will resent you for having hurt their pride, so you still will not have truly won them over. And nine times out of ten, the argument will only make the other person more entrenched in their stance than they were before. Therefore, the only solution is to avoid such disputes from the start.

The next time you encounter opposition to your ideas, do not start arguing to bolster your views, but instead try to accept the disagreement as something positive that brings a new perspective to your attention. After all, if two people always agree on everything, then one of them is dispensable. What is more, be sure to distrust the first response that bubbles up in you as it is usually an instinctively defensive one. And whatever you do, control your temper.

Listen to what your opponent has to say without resistance or protest and promise to carefully examine their thoughts. Try to find areas where you agree and dwell on these points while also freely admitting if you have made mistakes. This will help reduce your opponent's defensiveness. Then, thank your opponent. After all, you could just as easily see them as a friend who cares passionately about the topic at hand and wants to help you come to the right conclusion. Finally, propose to meet again later to allow both parties to think about it in the meantime. During this break, ask yourself if your opponent could be right and whether your reaction is likely to produce the results you seek. By keeping these points in mind, you can avoid unnecessary arguments.

SHY AWAY FROM TELLING OTHERS THEY ARE WRONG; THEY WILL ONLY RESENT YOU

Whenever you tell someone they are wrong, you are basically saying, "I'm smarter than you." This is a direct attack on their self-esteem, and they will want to retaliate because you are clearly disrespecting their opinions. So, whenever you want to express your opposition to someone's opinions, avoid absolute terms like "It is clear that..." or

"Obviously, the case is..." These telegraph the message "I'm smarter than you," and even if you do think you are smarter, you should never openly display this mentality.

If you want the other person to re-evaluate their view, it is much more effective to be humble and open-minded. You could say, for example, "I thought differently but I might be wrong. I've been wrong pretty often, so let us have a look at the facts again together." If you frame your opposition like this, the other person is much less likely to resist or resent you before giving you a chance to air your views. With a little luck, a soft approach will quickly turn opponents into allies, making it possible for you to change their opinions.

When you happen to be wrong yourself, step up and admit it right away. The truth is, we all make mistakes. And whenever you do and someone is about to berate you for it, there is an easy way to steal their thunder: admit your mistake. This helps because the other person was no doubt planning to bolster their own self-esteem by criticizing you about your mistake, but the moment you admit your guilt, the situation completely changes. Now, to feel important, they can no longer attack you, but rather must show generosity by forgiving you.

The next time you realize you are in the wrong, admit it enthusiastically. It will produce better results, and you will find it is much more enjoyable than having to defend yourself when the other person points out your mistake.

When you want to be convincing, start in a friendly way and get others to say "yes" as often as possible. Try to choose a simple strategy to accomplish this: friendliness and emphasize how proud and happy you are to meet them and how it was an important day in your life. Speak of them as dear friends with whom you have shared many interests. Friendliness can make people change their minds much more effectively than bluster and fury, so whatever it is you are trying to achieve, be sure to start in a friendly way.

Another important persuasion technique is getting people to say "yes" right from the start. Begin by emphasizing all the points on which you agree with the other person and ask questions that get them to say "yes" a lot. Think of it like building momentum in a billiard ball, it will be hard for them to reverse course after all those "yeses." On the other hand, you should avoid getting the other person to say "no," because they will be extremely reluctant to back away from this statement once made. And for people in sales, multiple "yeses" can translate into more sales.

The next time you feel like telling someone they are wrong, start in a friendly way and ask a gentle question that will get them to say "yes."

During moments where changing others needs to be done, start with praise and lavish them with more continuously. Here in lies an important lesson: just as a barber lathers a man's face before a shave to make the procedure more comfortable, so it is easier for us to hear unpleasant things after receiving praise. Keep this in mind whenever you wish for someone to make a change. Nor should you stop at the initial praise. Be sure to encourage the other person and praise them for every improvement they make, no matter how small. This will motivate them and make it seem easy for them to make the change you desire. People's abilities languish under criticism but bloom under encouragement. The next time you need to change someone's ways, be generous with your praise.

Circling back to admitting fault first, when drawing attention to mistakes do so indirectly and be sure to speak of your own errors first. To do this, even subtle changes to what you say can be enough. The next time you plan to start with praise but then say "...but..." and continue with the criticism, think about how you could formulate the criticism more softly with an "and." For example, instead of saying to your child: "Your grades are looking good, but your algebra is still lagging," try saying "Your grades are looking good, and if you keep working on your algebra, it'll soon catch up!" In addition to this indirect approach, you will find people more receptive if you begin by talking about your own mistakes.

Do your best to get "but" out of your language all together because the word "but" negates or cancels everything that goes before it. And is generally accepted as a signal that the important part of the sentence is coming up. When you use it, most people listening to you will give more attention and more weight to what you say after you say BUT. But by negating what the other person is saying, you begin to lose credibility with them.

NOTES:

CHAPTER 5

AUTHENCITY ABOVE ALL ELSE

"If you tell the truth you don't have to remember anything."
– Mark Twain

In this new age, you must do more than manage your career. You must act bravely and with "authenticity" in all social arenas of your life. This requires developing an understanding of each social setting that surrounds you. When you act authentically, you embrace different aspects of yourself depending on your context. Authentic leaders go beyond self-awareness to "selves awareness," which takes discipline, application, and skill. In our professional career we all go on our own journeys and transformations that develop our authenticity that also bleed over to our personal lives as well.

BEING AUTHENTIC MEANS BEING TRUE TO YOURSELF

Through history, people have reflected on the meaning of authenticity. Generally, they took the concept to mean the desire to live according to a personal set of values and beliefs. Has that definition changed? Well, the world around you may have changed. In the past, an authentic life often meant doing the same thing every day. When our specific industries dominated the economy, jobs and even careers were predictable. Finding the balance between being your true self and adapting to the discord of pressures is a complex, very personal equation.
Since 2000, several trends have shaped how people work:

- the popularity of smartphones
- the advent of social media
- the rapidity of marketplace change
- the deflation of hierarchical systems
- generational shifts at work
- a problematic job market, including layoffs and downsizing

Today you must do more than supervise your own career. You must act bravely and authentically. Authenticity captures the spirit of the 21st century. For instance, your clients and customers demand authenticity from the products they buy and the companies they patronize.

Which means the one question you should constantly be asking yourself is, what makes you different? The world was once described as a world dominated by average knowledge workers. It was suggested that workers should know their strengths and should figure out where they could contribute the most within a working framework defined by their principles. The concept of authenticity is inextricably linked with doing the right things and being a moral person in the real world. Authenticity is challenging because most people tell small lies and seldom reflect on their implications. Note when you are lying.

Think about the times when you lied. Stay aware of the difference between the telling the truth and telling a lie. Become aware of the emotions you feel when you lie. These moments are called standing in a lie. To become more authentic, you must accept and acknowledge when and why you have acted dishonestly. In the past, most people saw very few options when considered what work their jobs demanded. But the Internet revolution has led to a work world with less stratification and more fluid hierarchies.

In this new world, you have a wider array of career choices. To act authentically, you need to see the richness of your options. That is where the "the genius of the and" comes in. Outstanding companies do not get trapped in limited options, that is, the "tyranny of the or." They consider the wealth of possibilities that "and" offers them. Try emulating the behavior of musicians and artists throughout history: Figure out what your heart wants you to do and then pursue it.

THE DEAD-BUG VIEW OF THE TRUTH

You may often confront challenges in your private and professional life that have no straightforward solutions. When you address these issues or events, adopt a businesslike perception of honesty, falsehood, and authenticity. Leading authentically and by ferociously seeking the truth are full of this kind of subtlety, nuance, and the frustrating absence of black-and-white. Many people take a simplistic approach toward truth.

This attitude is called the "the dead-bug view of truth," suggesting that people equate telling the truth to what they do when they see a dead bug. They make a remark about it and forget it. However, most of the questions you encounter will be more complex than that. To become more authentic, abandon the dead-bug view of the truth. Embrace a nuanced view of the people and concerns you face daily.

One way of doing this is to not over value charisma. If you have had an unsettling experience with other people, consider what factors might have caused an issue. Perhaps you realized you misjudged someone. Or, at work you might have let a superior's charisma blind your choice of actions. Leaders with an ability to attract followers can build people's enthusiasm so they will do extraordinary things. What are you going to do if you are a leader who really does not know the answer or know what to do?

You must rely on others and solve the problem as a team. However, at least one standard-setting examination of leadership found that not all successful leaders have charisma. When analyzing the behavior of high-level executives, seeking common traits in leaders who led their firms to extraordinary achievements, it was found that being charismatic was an important trait in transformative leaders. Be careful whom you follow. Some people who seem to practice authenticity are really conducting a masquerade.

You have a range of conversations at work, often about lighter things, like the weather or good food. In your search for authenticity, try to make time for more substantive conversations with your boss and colleagues. Because it is critical that you have and engage in conversations that matter. Generate deeper discussions by asking more questions. Ask people where they came from; discuss their management style and their perception of their strengths and weaknesses. As you pay more attention to yourself and your superiors, you will come to understand people's preferences, like whether your bosses consider authenticity important.

A FIXED MINDSET VERSUS A GROWTH MINDSET

In the effort to explain authenticity, it is important to distinguish between two mind-sets. If you have a "fixed mind-set," you tend to look at life in a binary manner and believe you either have talents or you do not. But if you have a "growth mindset," you will believe that you can reach whatever goals you set if you put your mind to it. People with a growth mind-set tend to achieve greater success, think more highly of themselves and embrace their gifts. If you consider authenticity on a spectrum, you will find you have many choices between acting authentically and acting falsely. To deepen your capacity to behave authentically, develop a growth mind-set.

One thing does hold true and that is no one becomes more authentic automatically. As you develop authenticity, you will encounter internal and external challenges. Internally, you may have experiences that make acting authentically nerve-racking or difficult. Externally, your environment or company could impose rules requiring employees to act in a way the bosses consider appropriate. Most discussions of authenticity suggest that you have just oneself. That is incorrect.

People display different aspects of themselves depending on their context. As an authentic leader, you need to go beyond being yourself with no self-governance. Instead, act skillfully and gain awareness of your different selves, called "selves awareness". Different kinds of stimuli will bring out a variety of inner selves for you to discover and understand.

Even further, some people can change their behavior according to prevailing circumstances. These people are good at tapping into an inner psychological pattern called "self-monitoring." Those who can self-monitor tend to focus on how other people around them act. If others in the same setting behave a certain way, like with caution, so do they. It is seductive to think we can easily sort the good people and the bad people. By contrast, those who react less significantly to changing circumstance have a weaker ability to self-monitor. They respond to the outside world based on how they feel internally, not based on how those around them act.

Someone with a poor self-monitoring ability might speak bluntly amid caution people and thus undermine their effectiveness, authority, and credibility. Charisma can have a dark side, as some of the worst individuals in the history of the world could be described as charismatic. One challenge in the quest for authentic leadership is giving up the belief that you have only one unchangeable self.

Develop your talent for "balanced processing." Learn to examine your world without exaggerating the importance of your personal perspective. You will find it easier to learn balanced processing than to act as if you have no biases. Bias is part of human behavior, but self-aware people work beyond prejudices. Becoming skilled at balanced processing helps prevent self-deception and builds your awareness of how to respond to those around you.

AUTHENTIC LEADERSHIP REQUIRES CANDID HONESTY

Today's leaders need to create an atmosphere of honesty within their organizations. The culture they foster should encourage their colleagues to share information candidly. You cannot achieve authentic leadership without speaking honestly when necessary. Most people try to protect themselves at all costs. That is part of human nature. As an authentic leader, you must tell your people honestly how you expect them to behave. Set an example by acting with transparency. Many discussions of transparency suggest that individuals either act transparently or do not, which oversimplifies the issue. Most people lack genuine inner clarity. They cannot act the way they feel because they seldom know their true feelings.

The 21st century highlights the importance of transparency. The growth of social media enables people to share a lot of themselves and their lives. This new openness causes problems for people who act without sufficient self-protection. People tend to fall into the category of being too transparent or too blurred about their emotions. In the past, organizations behaved as if they functioned in isolation from community. They did not share internal information with the outside world.

Most leaders think about openness only in terms of their immediate circumstances. For instance, they might worry about what to say when they must fire someone. Instead, consider how you can help others understand you better. Sharing stories about a challenging period in your life will help people understand the effort you made to overcome your challenges. And hearing their stories will build your understanding of them.

When you decide to act transparently, keep in mind the social imperatives you need to follow and the persona you must create. In the past, people did not worry about ensuring that others consistently thought well of them. Their main concern was making enough money to survive. But in today's world, maintaining your image is a matter of paramount importance. Leaders must figure out how to navigate emotional transparency question themselves in a way that is true to who they are because what's right for one is not right for another.

The key question is, 'What's right for you?" The social hierarchy affects how people see each other. Those lower on the corporate ladder tend to exaggerate the power of those higher up. To present the right image in a hierarchical setting, you must follow socially mandated practices. However, stay mindful of the gap between any roleplaying and your real self. You will find discrepancies between the character you try to project and your true self. Do not let the divide get too wide.

Many high-level executives grumble that colleagues do not tell them the facts. Consider what would happen if everyone at work decided to take a "truth serum" that made them say exactly what they think. Most people believe such honesty would have a positive impact, but others worry that reacting with impulsive candor could have unfortunate results. As a leader, you can specify a set of norms for you and your colleagues to follow.

Embrace mistakes. Encourage the disclosure of negative news. People find negative information less threatening when they have clarity about their freedom to discuss it. Make becoming yourself a work of art. Be proactive, creative, and inventive. Look for opportunities to make signature contributions that only you could make. Leaders have an onerous responsibility. They must prove to their colleagues every day that they deserve trust. As a leader, accept that you make mistakes. When you let others know that you acknowledge this possibility, they will trust you more, not less.

NOTES:

CHAPTER 6

BECOME YOUR BIGGEST CHAMPION

"If you don't stand for something, you will fall for anything." – Alexander Hamilton

Are you living your best possible life? Put differently, are you thriving, or just surviving? That is a question that I often find myself asking more than I feel that I should. I have come to realize it is a question few of us can really answer with a resounding yes which is unfortunate. After all, being true to yourself and leading an authentic existence is not easy. How to be your best self might be the most important subject in the world, but neither parents nor schools usually teach us how to go about it.

If you want to change your life but are not sure where to start, this chapter on advocating is for you. Through deep reflection upon my own personal issues, struggles, and journey, the steps to finding your best self is packed full of actionable ideas you can start using today to put yourself on the path to a better tomorrow and it all starts with being your biggest advocate.

START DEFINING YOUR AUTHENTIC SELF

In a world full of bests, few people are taught how to be their best selves. "You're unique." It is a line you have probably heard a thousand times, but have you ever let it sink in? Nobody on Earth will know what it is like to walk in your shoes. Every thought, experience and feeling you have is yours alone; there has never been, and will never be, another you. Chances are, however, that you were never taught how to just be your best self.

You entered the world as a blank slate that has been drawn on like an artist on a canvas where people, starting with your parents, infringed their own successes, failures, and beliefs on. Then came grade school, friends, college, adulthood, and you get the picture. Sure, you learned all sorts of things, but what about connecting with who you really are? It is pretty much the most important skill in the world, but you will not find it on any curriculum.

The result is that we often end up leading lives which feel a little off. There is a vague sense we are not being our true selves, but we are not sure what to do about it. This means we must work hard to advocate for ourselves. We all have two types of self: a positive best self which is the person you would like to be more often and a negative anti-self which stops you being that person. The key is to learn to tell which self is in control. The best way to do that is to flesh out these characters and give them recognizable attributes.

You can start finding this out but looking at your best self. On a piece of paper, write down all your positive traits: the things you admire most about yourself but do not always act upon. Think of adjectives like "friendly," "logical" or "brave." That might be hard after all, it is much easier to criticize than praise yourself but stick with it. Next, put a face to that bundle of attributes. Does your best self-have a specific gender? Is it an animal or mythical creature? What is its superpower?

Once you have settled on your best self's appearance and character, you will want to sketch it. Do not worry, this does not have to be a masterpiece. The important thing is to have a representation to hang somewhere in your home to remind yourself of who you want to be. Next in this chapter we will take a closer look at your best self's nemesis that stands in the way of advocating for yourself: the anti-self.

GET YOUR NEGATIVE TRAITS UNDER CONTROL BY IDENTIFYING YOUR ANTI-SELF

Have you ever seen someone absolutely lose it while driving? I know I am certainly guilty of this. Road rage causes a remarkable Jekyll and Hyde transformation: the kindest, most considerate people in the world suddenly turn into raging road maniacs screaming at everyone around them. That is a pretty good example of someone's anti-self taking control. It is the part of your personality that responds to situations in the worst possible way, especially when triggers remind you of old wounds and fears. Being out of control and worrying about being late for work triggered that old anxiety.

The good news is that getting a clear idea of your anti-self gives you a much better chance of predicting when it is likely to rear its ugly head. Think back to the last time you acted in a way that later made you think "wow, I really lost it back there." Maybe you had an argument with a relative and hung up the phone. What you need to do is write down everything you do not like about your behavior when your anti-self is in charge. Use negative adjectives like "careless," "irrational" or "angry" to fill your list. Push past any sense of shame. Things look a lot scarier when they are lurking in the shadows, so think of this as taking a flashlight to the problem.

Now repeat what you did with your best self: put a name and a face to it. Remember, this is an exaggerated version of yourself, so do not be afraid to make this character cartoonish. In fact, the more ridiculous your portrait, the easier it will be to remember the behavior you want to avoid in the future. Think of several recent situations when your anti-self was in control. Write down how you behaved and then compare it to what your best self would have done. Keeping that in mind will help you step back and make better decisions when you are triggered rather than simply losing it.

Fear is the enemy of your best self, but it can be conquered with honesty. Advocating for yourself is a constant process which means becoming your best self is a continual journey. That means you will face obstacles along the way. If you want to reach your destination, you will need to avoid as many potholes and other hazards as possible. And the biggest obstacle you will encounter is fear.

The best way to overcome fear is to face up to it and be honest with yourself. Remember, fear is a habitual liar. It whispers in your ear that you are not good enough or that other people are judging you. Eventually, you end up with an entirely distorted view of the world and waste precious time and brainpower mulling over what-ifs. That means you will become so consumed by worries about hypotheticals that you will not get anything positive done. Think about fear as an acronym, False Evidence Appearing Real.

But here is the good news: there are a couple of simple strategies to put your fears into perspective. The first step is to identify them. Grab a pen and write out this question: "What are the fears that have held me back from making changes to my life?" Take a close look at your answers, is there an overarching theme? Are you terrified of failure, for example, or what people think about you? Now you are ready for the next step: putting your fears to the test. Like any other muscle, the brain can be trained. Negative thinking, however, usually means that you are focusing on fear, rather than solutions. What you need is an action plan to beat fear, and here is how.

Now write down these three headings: "My fear is," "It's keeping me from" and "My plan to stop my fear becoming reality is." Say you would love to quit your job and set up your own business, but the prospect of financial ruin is holding you back. One solution would be to put enough money away to tide you over for six months and only quitting your job once you have saved that amount.

Another great tool is visualization. Next time fear raises its ugly head, try out this technique. Close your eyes and imagine putting all your anxieties into a massive cardboard box. Now shrink that box in your mind's eye until it fits into the palm of your hand. Finally, picture yourself hurling that negative package into a deep, dark canyon and savor the feeling of relief that washes over you as you watch it drop out of sight.

EVEN INTROVERTS CAN LEARN TO SOCIALIZE AND BECOME THEIR BEST ADVOCATES

Everything we have talked about thus far in this chapter has been about advocating for yourself by focusing and being your best self but what about your relationships with others? After all, no person is an island of their own. Let us take a closer look at your social life, starting with why socializing is so important in the first place. All evidence points to the idea that socializing is great for your body and soul. Social interaction is basically like taking your brain to the gym. It is one of the best ways of keeping your cognitive capacities in top shape.

Studies show that people are happiest on days when they had spent several hours socializing. That goes to show how important it is to build time for friends and family into your schedule. But you should not just be hanging out with people you already know. There is nothing more stimulating than getting out there and making friends. After all, that is when you are most likely to pick up new ideas. Inspiration is not likely to strike when sitting alone on your couch.

Here is the rub: few of us are natural-born social butterflies and lots of us find socializing, particularly with people we do not know, awkward, especially natural born introverts. Luckily, there are a couple of tricks you can start using today to help you socialize next time you find yourself at a gathering, especially in a networking setting where you could advance your professional stance. One of the most common problems people face is struggling to find something to say.

We addressed some solutions if you happen to struggle with something to say in Chapter 4. An easy to remember remedy is you just need to prepare yourself by thinking over some of the things you have recently learned or experienced. That takes the pressure off to come up with something on the spot and gives you a nice conversation opener. Paying attention to small details also makes a huge difference. Asking questions and listening attentively encourages people to be open as well. Then there's also body language. It is estimated that nonverbal cues account for a good sixty percent of all communication, so standing up straight, keeping your arms unfolded and making eye contact are great ways of showing that you are present and engaged.

BEFORE YOU CAN HELP OTHERS, YOU HAVE TO HELP YOURSELF

A lot of your most important relationships put you in the role of a care giver, nurturer, and helper. Looking out for others is a key part of becoming your best self and advocating. But that is only going to happen if you are taking care of yourself. Fail to do that and you just will not have the physical or emotional energy to be useful to anyone. Self-care, in other words, is not selfish, it is what allows you to give to others. That means it is vital to learn how to manage the stress and hustle-bustle of everyday life.

Let us look at some ways you can use to keep yourself healthy and well-balanced.

One technique to live by is mindful breathing. I have resisted this suggestion for many years until I recently caved into it and found it does work. One of the first things that happens when you are feeling overwhelmed is that your breathing becomes more rapid. Stepping back and taking three or four deep breaths is a great way to calm your stressed-out mind and put things back into perspective. Another great stress buster is exercise. Aim to spend at least twenty to thirty minutes each day working out. That can mean a brisk walk around the block, a bike ride, or a session in the gym, the key is to take your mind off things and get your blood pumping.

Next on the list and right up as one of if not the single most important aspect, sleep. A good night's rest is essential for your cognitive performance and overall body's ability to simply function. Make sure you are getting at least six hours of sleep each night and remember there is no making up for lost sleep so just do your best to get back on track when you veer off. Keep your bedtime regular and avoid eating and drinking carbonated or sweet beverages just before sleep. You also need passions to make your life meaningful and joyous.

Sure, finding time help take care of yourself is tricky, but it can be done, even when you are regularly grinding out long days in the office. Ultimately it is simple, do not take care of yourself and you will not be able to take care of anyone else either. The best way of finding out where to fit your hobby in your everyday life is to ask yourself what it is that stops you from, for example, painting the next Picasso or taking a walk in the park. Could you cut down on TV time or use your commute to listen to an audio course? As we have talked about, do not just focus on being efficient, focus more on being effective.

When we take a further dive into advocating for us, we also must look at other pain points when dealing with people and leaving with an impression of "it's complicated." It is a common enough phrase, but it is downright misleading. The truth is that many of the issues you will face in your relationships come down to a simple issue: unrealistic expectations. It is not surprising that so many of us have such misguided views. We are constantly bombarded by idealized depictions of love in movies, commercials, and music. Just think of the standard summer blockbuster: there will usually be plenty of romance and passion but very little of the bad moods, midlife crises and rough patches which are part and parcel of long-term relationships.

NOTES:

CHAPTER 7

DON'T JUST TALK ABOUT IT, BE ABOUT IT

"Trust takes years to build, seconds to break, and forever to repair." – Dhar Mann

The largest basis of all trust comes down to honest communication. As soon as we are caught in a lie, our credibility plummets. Above all else, to build trust in relationships, it is a must to be honest. Trust is ultimately defined as a belief in a person or thing. It indicates that a person or a product possesses inherent integrity, even in trying circumstances. Without trust, a business cannot forge new associations, retain employees, or enhance its customers' regard for its merchandise or services. This chapter provides insights to understand why your ability to get others to trust you is your greatest business and personal asset.

THE IMPORTANCE OF TRUST

Most people value trust over anything else. In the absence of trust, they find it difficult to do anything significant. That includes completing commercial transactions, affecting other people's opinions, working with other individuals, building the value of your brand, or increasing profitability. Trust is not a soft skill. It is a measurable competency that brings dramatic results. It can be built into a person or organization's strategy, goals, and culture.

Mistrust doubles the cost of doing business. Companies with high degrees of trust have profit levels almost three times above those with low trust. Conditions that encourage commercial transactions require trust and dissipate without it. Businesses cannot forge new associations or boost customers' regard. Without trust, an organization's ability to work effectively decreases, and its employee retention suffers.

Trust is a belief in a person or thing. Being trusted indicates that a person or a product has an inherent integrity even under the most trying circumstances. Strong trust connections are implicit. Your chair does not need to reassure you about its trustworthiness to encourage you to sit down. Similarly, trust in you or your organization speaks an implicit agreement that you will do as you promise. Greater trust brings superior innovation, creativity, freedom, morale, and productivity.

Industry leading businesses and leading executives have one thing in common, trust. It enables them to overcome rough patches, retain customer loyalty and price their products higher. Having customers who feel an unquestioning faith in your company and brand is a major strategic advantage. Trust is also palpable and quantifiable, and you can learn how to earn and elicit it. Getting people to trust you requires consistent adherence to a set of values and actions. You cannot achieve trust by merely acting polished or by exercising dishonesty.

THE VALUE OF TRUST

When it comes to organizations, hiring managers often fail to pay sufficient attention to the most important qualifications job applicants need: trust and trustworthiness. Trust is not just one element in a bouquet of leadership assets though. Trust is the foundation supporting everything you and your organization seek to accomplish. As you build trustworthiness, you will find that your colleagues and people outside your organization become increasingly willing to assist you.

Most sales executives could not get into a prospect's door if they were not trustworthy. I vividly remember immediately after graduating high school I answered an ad in the local newspaper seeking "sports marketing professionals" and I answered the call. I went right away, and it turned out to be door to door marketing selling golf memberships in local neighborhoods. Never did I think I would ever do such a thing, but it was so eye-opening as total strangers engaged with me and even let me into their home without knowing who I was or anything about me.

Yet for most sales executives they spend more time thinking about the latest sales technique than they do about how to build trust and ensure they are trustworthy. Organizations that embrace trust and reflect trust in every association gain increased profitability because trust is the natural result of thousands of tiny actions, words, thoughts, and intentions.

What I have found is that for most customers, they tend to forgive businesses they trust. In the aviation industry for example, customers trust Southwest Airlines. Despite the industry's economic pressures, Southwest has enjoyed consistent profitability for close to four decades. Early in 2008, however, it became clear that Southwest had let safety standards slide. It operated several aircrafts that should not have been in the air. When this came to light, the airline grounded the planes and fired the employees identified as responsible for this situation. Sometime later, a media outlet examined passengers' sentiment. Most passengers felt no resentment against Southwest because they felt nobody really cared about them

There are obstacles that you face when it comes to trust that you must be aware of. There are a lot of consumers that are feeling less trust in companies than they did fifteen years ago. Several factors erode trust, including, for example, conflicts of interest, such as those between equity holders and corporate management or between everyday citizens and politicians. Many other areas of life show a precipitous loss in respect for trust. Governments have even introduced legal frameworks that show some of these obstacles, such as the 2001 Patriot Act and the 2002 Sarbanes-Oxley Act, to ensure good behavior.

SEEK FORGIVENESS

If you act shabbily toward someone, you must accept the obligation to set the situation straight. Be sure that you act judiciously since early action facilitates a difficult situation.

To repair your reputation and regain people's confidence, make and, more important, keep small commitments. Because nowadays we know more about how to destroy trust than we do about it and how to build it.

Sometimes you could have acted so outrageously that the people you hurt may find it hard to forgive you. Make a heartfelt apology and do everything you can to rectify the situation. You may have to accept that you cannot do anything anymore. In the case of a company recovering from a serious error, consider if it would help to change its public symbols, such as the logo or name. While it may appear to be static, trust is more like a forest as a long time growing, but easily burned down with a touch of carelessness.

Your ability to inspire trust is your greatest asset and thus can make a significant impact. Commanding trust is a challenge for any business. Gaining it confers a huge advantage. There are no short cuts. You earn trust only if you act ethically. To build trust in your personal life and in every part of your business, you must adhere to a set of tenants that are relevant, proven, and timeless.

ESTABLISH THE DOCTRINES OF TRUST

Clarity is a means of speaking plainly and by doing so creates a bond; it encourages and engenders trust. When you speak clearly, you help build employee morale and engagement. Being easy to understand reduces discord between you and your employees or customers. Those who believe in trust do not beat around the bush. Google's success comes in part from its clear definition of its goals. It seeks to systematize all information so everyone can use its features productively. Everything it does reflects that mission.

Compassion is your ability to care and leads people to trust you. To enhance your capacity for compassion, consciously pay attention when others speak, praise them and work on their behalf. Strive for honesty and prioritize people over material goods. When it comes to your character, people's integrity and morality shapes their character. Integrity means a willingness to speak and live by certain norms without exception. But consistency is not enough.

You need relevant, current skills in your area of expertise to win trust and this is called competency. It means you have the wisdom to recognize when you need to upgrade your skills. When it comes to those who stick with you through the hard times and you show you loyalty, that is a major tenant called commitment. Several years ago, I faced the most difficult period of my personal and professional life and at a time when I needed people the most, especially my "professional friends" they were nowhere to be found. While for a decade plus prior I was at or near the top of the mountain, against so many odds when I had nothing to offer at that moment they fled, and it was devastating.

When you use trust to measure how you feel about the people and organizations in your life it forms your connection. Take a survey of random people and you will find that they will trust the suggestions of a friend over those of a critic. To generate trust, reach out. Reaching out to others requires making conversation, and to stimulate good conversations, you need to ask questions. Show interest in people and aspects of their life that are not part of your routines and habits. Behave in ways that reflect the real you.

To attain trust, do what you promise, and this forms contribution. The seeds of trust are the small promises you make and keep. You will receive more trust as you grant more trust. Make sure your actions have an impact that aligns with your overall vision. People who contribute bring out the best in others. They keep their promises and address crucial issues before taking on matters of less importance. They seek the right balance in paying attention to people and to work.

Finally, here, consistency. It is the easiest and most difficult aspect that ties everything mentioned above together. Act the same way, every time, in all circumstances, to good purpose. Consistency leads to trust. Deliver the same thing every time, and you will become trusted. The track record of trust is built over time. There is no other way to lasting success.

THINK GLOBALLY, ACT LOCALLY

Businesspeople must work with the globalization of commerce. When they seek new markets abroad or at home, they must earn trust to succeed. For example, business etiquette in various countries in Asia differs from the right etiquette in the United States. The differences may seem minor, but if you ignore them, you could upset your Asian counterpart. Many Asian communities value restraint. Your Asian associates will appreciate your efforts to conform to local practice. You will never get one big chance to be trusted in your life; you will get thousands of small ones.

So, what can you do to think globally and act locally? Try to learn a country's customs before you visit. When you are abroad, practice humility, pay attention, speak softly, express gratitude and restrain yourself until you understand the kinds of behaviors that the region's etiquette sanctions.

Today, many universities and businesses commonly promote the importance of diversity but having a broad mix of people of various types and nationalities might not encourage confidence. Most individuals tend to trust those with similar backgrounds. This does not apply necessarily to race and other ethnic factors, but to the nature of another person's personality or beliefs.

When you seek to increase trust, consider the impact of this affinity. Work to build trust with people one-on-one instead of relying on preconceived classifications. If you find you have differences with someone else because of your social background, strive for honesty. Shed social pretenses or artifice, and let people see you without any camouflage. This affinity can be applied to every aspect of human existence.

LIVE AND BREATHE TRUST

As people use the internet as their main source of communication, their perceptions change quickly. Most people believe the word of their friends and relatives more than they believe ads. Make sure your corporate and personal "online image" remains unsullied if you face a sudden attack on your good name. Follow these tips to build trust online:

Strive for clarity by emulating the simplicity of Google's site. Remove unnecessary clutter, and make sure your audience can easily understand who you are and what your offering. Provide information to resolve customer challenges. Be easily reachable by enhancing your customer's trust by providing several contact methods. Display a telephone number for consumers to use to call or text you, and make sure someone answers it. Even ensuring an email address is prominently located will add a layer of trust that will go a long way.

Make sure you give your website authenticity and provide pictures of actual customers and recommendations from your clients. Images of employees, locations and consumers add to your trustworthiness, much more than stock images that can be used by anyone. Look to join worthy charitable organizations as well, and link to them on your website. Include a page of frequently asked questions and be sure to acknowledge the questions you receive and respond swiftly while reaching out to established customers on a regular basis.

It is also important to send information to your new customers. Show them they made the right decision when they decided to follow or bought from you. But be sure to provide the latest information to them and when at all possible avoid excessive advertising on your website. This is not to say not to advertise if that is a source of you being able to do what you are called to do, but try and find other advertising methods that do not clutter your website. No matter what, make sure you value and always keep your website's visitors and customer's information safe and secure. This continues to become an increasingly crucial issue for customers and one security breach could be the last visit they make to you.

NOTES:

CHAPTER 8

WE ARE WHAT WE REPEATEDLY DO

"Watch your thoughts, they become your words; watch your words, they become your actions; watch your actions, they become your habits; watch your habits, they become your character; watch your character, it becomes your destiny." – Lao Tzu

Have you ever asked yourself the question, what is in it for me? Once the dust settles, that is ultimately what habits and achieving your goals is all about. In this chapter we are going to discuss how even the smallest habits can have a big impact on your life. To figure out how many habits you have, you might need a minute to think about that question, because habits are, by definition, behaviors that we perform automatically, with little or no thought. From making a cup of coffee when we get up in the morning to brushing our teeth before bed at night, our habits subtly guide our daily lives.

As a result, you may not realize how much strength there is in habits. If repeated every day, even the smallest actions, from saving a dollar to not drinking that extra can of Mr. Pibb, can accumulate force and have a huge effect. So, understanding and embracing habits is a great way to take control of your life and achieve more. As we continue to discuss, you will learn precisely what habits are, how they are formed and how you can harness them to change your life for the better.

SMALL HABITS HAVE A LARGE IMPACT ON YOUR LIFE

Imagine a plane taking off from Los Angeles in route to New York. If, during takeoff, the pilot decided to adjust course even a few degrees to the south, the plane's nose would move just a few feet. Outside of the cockpit, no one on board would notice the small movement. But over the course of a journey across the country, the impact of the change would be considerable, and the confused passengers would depart from their plane in Washington, DC, not New York.

We do not notice tiny changes, because their immediate impact is negligible. If you are out of shape today, and go for a 20-minute jog, you will still be out of shape tomorrow. Conversely, if you eat a family-size pizza for dinner, it will not make you overweight overnight. But if we repeat small behaviors day after day, our choices compound into major results. Eat pizza every day, and it is likely you will have gained considerable weight after a year. Go jogging for 20 minutes every day, and you will eventually be leaner and fitter, even though you will not have noticed the change happening.

If you want to make a positive change in your life, you must recognize that change requires patience, as well as confidence that your habits are keeping you on the right trajectory, even if you aren't seeing immediate results. So, if you find that your behaviors and habits do not seem to be paying off, try to focus on your current trajectory rather than your current results. If you have little money in the bank but you are saving something each month, then you can be confident that your trajectory is right.

Your current results might not be great, but keep going in this direction and, in a few months or a few years, you will notice a major improvement. By contrast, a millionaire who outspends his earnings each month may not be worried about his bank statements from one month to the next, but, in the end, his trajectory will catch up with him. The key to making big changes in your life does not have to involve major upheaval; you do not need to revolutionize your behavior or reinvent yourself. Rather, you can make tiny changes to your behavior, which, when repeated time and time again, will become habits that may lead to big results.

One of the most interesting things I have personally found when studying habits is that they are ultimately automated behaviors that we have learned from experiences. When you walk into a dark room, you do not think about what to do next; you instinctively reach for a light switch. It is a habit, a behavior that you have repeated so many times that it now happens automatically. When you back out of your driveway, you instinctively just back out and start going without realizing what took place. It stems from a subject my friend and leadership guru Brian Nieves could write and entire book on, "The Captain and the Crew" otherwise known as the conscious and subconscious mind.

Habits are formed by our brain figuring out how to respond to new situations through a process of trial and error. Once discovered, these behaviors give satisfying consequences, in some cases, gaining freedom that tends to be repeated until they become automatic. Still today, we continue to stumble across satisfying solutions to life's difficulties and predicaments. And, thankfully, we now understand a little more about how habits work.

You see, habits begin with a cue, or a trigger to act. Walking into a dark room cues you to perform an action that will enable sight. Next comes a craving for a change in state, in this case, to be able to see. Then comes our response, or action, flicking the light switch. The final step in the process, and the end goal of every habit, is the reward. Here, it is the feeling of mild relief and comfort that comes from being able to see your surroundings.

Every habit is subject to the same process. Do you habitually drink coffee every morning? Waking up is your cue, triggering a craving to feel alert. Your response is to drag yourself out of bed and make a k-cup of Dunkin Donuts coffee. Your reward is feeling alert and ready to face the world. But, of course, not all habits are good for us. Now that we understand how habits work, let us look at building positive ones that improve our lives.

NEW HABITS REQUIRE A PLAN OF ACTION AND HARD-TO-MISS CUES

All of us have cues that trigger certain habits. The buzz of your phone, for example, is a cue to check your messages. And once you understand that certain stimuli can prompt habitual behavior, you can use this knowledge to change your habits. One way is to change your surroundings and general environment to encourage better habits. Very simple changes to our environment can make a big difference. Want to practice guitar? Leave the instrument out in the center of the room. Trying to eat healthier snacks? Leave them out on the counter, instead of in the refrigerator drawer. Make your cues as obvious as possible, and you will be more likely to respond to them.

A second great way to strengthen cues is to use implementation intentions. Most of us tend to be too vague about our intentions. We say, "I'm going to eat better," and simply hope that we will follow through. An implementation intention introduces a clear plan of action, setting out when and where you will carry out the habit you would like to cultivate. Look at voters in the United States, when they are asked questions like "At what time will you vote?" and "How will you get to the voting station?" were more likely to actually turn out than those who were just asked if they would vote.

So, do not just say, "I'll run more often." Say, "On Monday, Wednesday and Friday, when the alarm goes off, the first thing I'll do is put my running gear and run two miles." Then leave your running shoes out where you will see them, even trip over them if necessary. You will be giving yourself both a clear plan and an obvious cue, and it may surprise you how much easier this will make it to build a positive running habit.

There is one thing that as humans we cannot deny, we are motivated by the anticipation of reward. Which means making habits attractive will help you stick to them. In our history, there have been experiments to test the neurology of desire. Using electrodes, they blocked the release of the neurotransmitter dopamine in lab animals. To their surprise, those animals simply lost the will to live. They had no desire to eat, drink, reproduce or do anything else. Mere days later, they all died of thirst.

The human brain also releases dopamine, a hormone that makes us feel good, when we do pleasurable things such as eating or having sex. But we also get a hit of feel-good dopamine when we simply anticipate those pleasurable activities. It is the brain's way of driving us onward and encouraging us to do things. So, in the brain's reward system, desiring something is on par with getting something, which goes a long way toward explaining why kids enjoy the anticipation of Christmas so much. It is also why daydreaming about your upcoming hot date is so pleasurable.

We can also turn this knowledge to our advantage when trying to form habits. If we make a habit something we look forward to, we will be much more likely to follow through and do it. A great technique for this is temptation bundling. That is when you take a behavior that you think of as important but unappealing and link it to a behavior that you are drawn to, one that will generate that motivating dopamine hit.

Take for example a person who knows they need to exercise more, but they get little enjoyment from working out. However, they did enjoy binge watching the latest Netflix's Ozark Season 3 and other shows. So, they hacked an exercise bike, connecting it to their laptop and writing code that would only allow Netflix to run if they were cycling at a certain speed. By linking exercise, literally, to a behavior that they were naturally drawn to, they transformed a distasteful activity into a pleasurable one.

You also do not need to be an engineer to apply this to your life. If you need to work out, but you want to catch up on the latest sport scores, you could commit to only reading the latest sport websites and apps while at the gym. If you want to watch the latest news and scores, but you need to make sales calls, promise yourself an hour of ESPN after you talk to your seventh prospect of the day. Soon enough, you may even find those unattractive tasks enjoyable since you will be anticipating a pleasing reward while carrying them out.

TO ADOPT A NEW HABIT, MAKE IT EASY TO BUILD

We often spend a lot of time on behaviors that are easy. Scrolling through social media, for example, takes zero effort, so it is easy for it to fill up lots of our time. Doing several diamond art paintings like my youngest daughter Sophia or studying German like my middle daughter Abby, in contrast, requires a lot of effort and attention repeating those behaviors daily until they become habitual is tough. So, making behaviors as easy as possible is key to turning them into habits. Luckily, there are a few tricks you can embrace to make anything seem easier. The first is to focus on reducing friction.

The less friction you have in front of a habit, the more likely it is you will accomplish it. Here are a few approaches to increase friction for bad habits. If you want to waste less time in front of the TV, unplug it and take the batteries out of the remote. Doing so will introduce enough friction to ensure you only watch when you really want to.

The second trick for making a habit easier in the long term is the two-minute rule, a way to make any new activity feel manageable. The principle is that any activity can be distilled into a habit that is doable within two minutes. Want to read more? Do not commit to reading one book every week, instead, make a habit of reading two pages per night. Want to run a marathon? Commit to simply putting on your running gear every day after you get home from work.

The two-minute rule is an effective and simple way to build easily achievable habits, and those can lead you on to greater things. Once you have put on your running shoes, you will probably head out for a run. Once you have read two pages, you will likely finish a chapter. The rule recognizes that simply getting started is the first and most important step toward doing something. Making your habits immediately satisfying is essential to effective behavior change.

One of the most important rules for behavioral change is to make habits satisfying. This can be difficult, for evolutionary reasons. Today, we live in what academics call a delayed-return environment. You turn up at the office today, but the return, a paycheck, does not come until the end of the month. You go to the gym in the morning, but you do not lose weight overnight. Our brains, though, evolved to cope with the immediate-return environment of earlier humans, who were not thinking about long-term returns like saving for retirement or sticking to a diet.

They were focused on immediate concerns like finding their next meal, seeking shelter, and staying alert enough to escape any nearby lions. Immediate returns can encourage bad habits, too. Smoking may give you lung cancer in twenty years, but, in the moment, it relieves your stress and the craving for nicotine, which means you may ignore the long-term effects and indulge in a cigarette. So, when you are pursuing habits with a delayed return, try to attach some immediate gratification to them. However pleasurable and satisfying we make habits; we may still fail to maintain them.

Whether you are trying to write in your journal or give up smoking, managing your own behaviors can be hard. Create a framework to keep your habits on track by using trackers and contracts. Thankfully, there are a few simple measures that can help. Habit tracking is a simple but effective technique. Many people have kept a record of their habits; one of the most well-known is founding father Benjamin Franklin. From a very young age, Franklin kept a notebook in which he recorded adherence to thirteen personal virtues, which included aims like avoiding frivolous conversation and to always be doing something useful. He noted his success every night.

You, too, can develop a habit tracker, using a simple calendar or diary, and crossing off every day that you stick with your chosen behaviors. You will find it effective because habit tracking itself is an attractive and satisfying habit. The anticipation and action of crossing off each day will feel good and keep you motivated.

Another technique is to develop a habit contract that imposes negative consequences if you fail to stay on track. Humans are social animals. We care about the opinions of those around us, so simply knowing that someone is watching you can be a powerful motivator for success. So why not set yourself a habit contract? Even if it is not significantly detailed, consider making a commitment to your spouse, your best friend or one of your coworkers. If you agree upon a set of consequences for failing to follow through, you will be much more likely to stick to your habits. And as we have seen, sticking to a positive habit, however small, is a surefire way to achieve big things in life.

NOTES:

CHAPTER 9

FOCUS ON THE EXECUTION

"The secret of getting ahead is getting started." – Tim Cook

Too many people fool themselves into thinking they or their companies are a well-oiled machine. The fundamental problem is that people think of execution as just a tactical side, something they delegate while they focus on the perceived "bigger" issues. This idea is completely wrong. Execution is not just tactics but rather it is a discipline and a system. It must be built into your strategy, goals, and culture.

As a leader, you are already deeply engaged in your personal life, but you must be in your organization's as well. Many leaders often fall victim to the gap between promises they have made and results their organizations have delivered. They frequently tell how they have a problem with accountability, people are not doing the things they are supposed to do to implement a plan. They desperately want to make changes of some kind, but what do they need to change? They do not know. Execution is a specific set of behaviors that once addressed and changed is a difference maker.

THE GAP NOBODY KNOWS

When individuals and companies fail to deliver on their promises, the most frequent explanation is that the leader's strategy was wrong. But the strategy by itself is not often the cause. Strategies most often fail because they are not executed well. Things that are supposed to happen do not happen. Either the responsible party is not capable of making them happen, or the leaders of the organization misjudged the challenges faced in the current environment, or both. The gap nobody knows is the gap between what leaders want to achieve and the ability of them and their organization to achieve it.

Everybody like talks about change, we even dedicate a whole chapter to it in this book. In recent years, a small industry of change-meisters had preached revolution, reinvention, quantum change, breakthrough thinking, audacious goals, learning organizations, and the like. We are not necessarily debunking this stuff. But unless you translate big thoughts into concrete steps for action, they are pointless. Without execution, the breakthrough thinking breaks down, learning adds no value, people do not meet their stretch goals, and the revolution stops dead in its tracks.

What you get is change for the worse because failure drains the energy from everyone. Repeated failure destroys it. Nobody can deliver on its commitments or adapt well to change unless all leaders practice the discipline of execution at all levels. Execution must be a part of everyone's strategy and its goals. If you do not know how to execute, the whole of your effort as a leader will always be less than the sum of its parts.

To understand execution, you must keep three key points in mind:

1. Execution is a discipline, and integral to strategy.
2. Execution is the major job of the leader.
3. Execution must be a core element of a culture.

No worthwhile strategy can be planned without considering the ability to execute it. Otherwise, execution is a systematic way of exposing reality and acting on it. The heart of execution lies in the three core processes: the people process, the strategy process, and the operations process.

Lots of people like to think that the head person in charge is exempt from the details of running things. It is a pleasant way to view leadership: you stand on the mountaintop, thinking strategically and attempting to inspire your people with visions, while managers do the grunt work. An organization can execute only if the leader's heart and soul are immersed in the company. The leader must oversee getting things done by running the three core processes: picking other leaders, setting the strategic direction, and conducting operations.

Only a leader can ask the tough questions that everyone needs to answer, then manage the process of debating the information and making the right trade-offs. And only the leader who is intimately engaged in the business can know enough to have the comprehensive view and ask the touch incisive questions. Dialogue is the core of culture and the basic unit of work. How people talk to each other absolutely determines how well the organization will function. Everyone likes to say that people are the most important ingredient in their success. But they often hand off the job of assessing people and rewarding them to the HR staff, then rubber-stamp the recommendations at their reviews. Only true leaders who know the people can make the right judgments.

Good judgments come from practice and experience. But there is an enormous difference between leading an organization and presiding over it. The leader who boasts of their hands-off style or puts her faith in empowerment is not dealing with the issues of the day. They are not confronting the people responsible for poor performance or searching for problems to solve and then making sure they get solved. They are presiding, and they are only doing half their job. Leading for execution is not about micromanaging or being "hands-on," or disempowering people. Rather, it is about active involvement and doing the things leaders should be doing in the first place.

The leader who executes effectively ultimately assembles an architecture of it. They put in place a culture and processes for executing, promoting people who get things done more efficiently and giving them greater rewards. Leaders of this type are powerful and influential presences because they are their businesses. They are intimately and intensely involved with their people and operations. They connect because they know the realities and talk about them. They are knowledgeable about the details. They are excited about what they are doing. They are passionate about getting results. This is not "inspiration" through exhortation or speechmaking. These leaders energize everyone by the example they set.

EXECUTION HAS TO BE IN THE CULTURE

Leaders who execute look for deviations from desired managerial tolerances which is the gap between the desired and actual outcome in everything from profit margins to the selection of people for promotion. Then they move to close the gap and raise the bar still higher across the whole organization. The intellectual challenge of execution is in getting to the heart of an issue through persistent and constructive probing. The intellectual challenge of execution is in getting to the heart of an issue through persistent and constructive probing

Are the right people in charge of getting it done and is their accountability clear are two powerful questions you as a leader must be asking? Whose collaboration will be required, and how will they be motivated to collaborate? Will the reward system motivate them to a common objective? In other words, the leader does not just sign off on a plan. They want an explanation, and they will drill down until the answers are clear. Organizations do not execute unless the right people, individually and collectively, focus on the right details as the right time.

What exactly does a leader who oversees execution do? How do they keep from being a micromanager, caught up in the details of running the business? Here are the building blocks in the foundation of execution:

- Know your people and your business

- Insist on realism
- Set clear goals and priorities
- Follow through
- Reward the doers
- Expand people's capabilities
- Know yourself

Leaders must live their businesses. Being present allows you, as a leader, to connect personally with your people, and personal connections help you build your intuitive feel for the business as well as for the people running the business. They also help to personalize the mission you are asking people to perform. Sometimes the leaders are simply in denial. When we ask leaders to describe their organization's strengths and weaknesses, they generally state the strengths well, but they are not so good on identifying the weaknesses. And when we ask what they are going to do about the weaknesses, the answer is rarely clear or cohesive. You start by being realistic yourself. Always insist on realism because sometimes people are simply in denial.

Leaders who execute focus on a few clear priorities that everyone can grasp. First, anybody who thinks through the logic of a business will see that focusing on three or four priorities will produce the best results from the resources at hand. Second, people in contemporary organizations need a small number of clear priorities to execute well. A leader who says "I've got priorities" does not know what they are talking about as they do not know themselves what the most important things are. You have got to have these few, clearly realistic goals and priorities, which will influence the overall performance of the company.

Another thing you will notice about leaders who execute is that they speak simply and directly. They talk plainly and forthright about what is on their minds. They know how to simplify things so that others can understand them, evaluate them, and act on them, so that what they say becomes common sense. If you want people to produce specific results, you reward them accordingly. This fact seems so obvious that it should not need saying. Yet many leaders do such a poor job of linking rewards to performance that there's little correlation at all. They do not distinguish between those who achieve results and those who do not either in base pay or in bonuses and stock options. It is very important to reward the doers. If you want people to produce specific results, you reward them accordingly.

The inability to act decisively which translates into an inability to execute is rooted in the culture and seems to be impervious to change. The key word here is "seems," because, in fact, leaders create a culture of indecisiveness, and leaders can break it. Structure divides an organization into units designed to perform certain jobs. You should not expect people to know everything, but we do expect people to get the best answers they can get, and they get them by working with other people.

ROBOST DIALOGUE IS IMPORTANT

You cannot have an execution culture without robust dialogue. Robust dialogue starts when people go in with open minds. They are not trapped by preconceptions or armed with a private agenda. They want to hear new information and choose the best alternatives, so they listen to all sides of the debate and make their own contributions. When people speak candidly, they express their real opinions, not those that will please the power players or maintain harmony. Formality suppresses dialogue; informality encourages it. Formal conversations and presentations leave little room for debate. They suggest that everything is scripted and predetermined. Informal dialogue is open. It invites questions, encouraging spontaneity and critical thinking.

Informality gets the truth out. Robust dialogue also ends with closure. At the end of the meeting, people agree about what each person must do and when. They have committed to it in an open forum; they are accountable for the outcomes. Think about the meetings you have attended that were a hopeless waste of time and those that produced energy and great results. What was the difference? The difference was in the quality of the dialogue. Dialogue alters the psychology of a group. It can either expand a group's capacity or shrink it. It can be energizing or energy-draining. It can create self-confidence and optimism, or it can produce pessimism. It can create unity, or it can create bitter factions. Robust dialogue brings out reality, even when that reality makes people uncomfortable, because it has purpose and meaning.

Leaders do tend to get the behavior they exhibit and tolerate because the culture of a company is the behavior of its leaders. Let us say it again, "leaders get the behavior they exhibit and tolerate." You measure the change in culture by measuring the change in the personal behavior of its leaders and the performance of the business.

Having the right people in the right place given the many things that we can't control, from the uncertain state of the economy to the unpredictable actions of competitors, you'd think companies would pay careful attention to the one thing they can control which is the quality of their people, especially those in the leadership pool. An organization's human beings are its most reliable resource for generating excellent results year after year. Their judgments, experiences, and capabilities make the difference between success and failure.

We notice, these leaders do not pay enough attention to people because they are too busy thinking about how to make their companies bigger or more global than those of their competitors. What they are overlooking is that the quality of their people is the best competitive differentiator. Over time, choosing the right people is what creates that elusive status and sustainable competitive advantage. If you look at any business that is consistently successful, you will find that its leaders focus intensely and relentlessly on people selection.

The question is then why aren't the right people in the right jobs? Common sense tells us the right people must be in the right jobs. Yet so often they are not. What accounts for the mismatches you see every day? The leaders may not know enough about the people they are appointing. They may pick people with whom they are comfortable, rather than others who have better skills for the job. They may not have the courage to discriminate between strong and weak performers and take the necessary actions. All of these reflect one fundamental shortcoming: The leaders are not personally committed to the people process and deeply engaged in it.

Once you have finally decided to execute and execute consistently, just as important is your follow through. Follow-through is the cornerstone of execution, and every person who is good at executing follows through religiously. Never finish a meeting without clarifying what the follow-through will be, who will do it, when and how they will do it, what resources they will use, and how and when the next review will take place and with whom. And never launch an initiative unless you are personally committed to it and prepared to see it through until it is embedded in the DNA of an organization.

It is the people of an organization who make judgments about how markets are changing, create strategies based on those judgments, and translate the strategies into operational realities. A robust people process does three things. It evaluates individuals accurately and in depth. It provides a framework for identifying and developing the leadership talent. It fills the leadership pipeline that is the basis of a strong succession plan. Very few companies accomplish all these objectives well. One of the biggest shortcomings of the traditional people process is that it is backward-looking, focused on evaluating the jobs people are doing today. Far more important is whether the individuals can handle the jobs of tomorrow.

Too often people wait until the results are in before making corrections in key leadership positions. By then, the damage is done. Types of decisions like putting the wrong people in place to execute a key part of a business's strategy are common. Whether they are expanding a new location or launching a new service or product, far too many leaders do not ask the most basic questions: Who are the people who are going to execute that strategy, and can they do it?

NOTES:

CHAPTER 10

CHANGE-MAKER

"The measure of intelligence is the ability to change." –
Albert Einstein

WHEN CREATING CHANGE, CREATE URGENCY

The first step for leaders when it comes to handling change is to create a sense of urgency. This is a series of actions that leaders take to communicate with critical stakeholders why change must occur and why it must occur now.

One way to view this step is to see it as an opening argument. For change leaders, creating a sense of urgency is like what an attorney does in court in his or her opening argument. The attorney uses information and facts to get the court's attention and make a compelling argument for their position. Change leaders do this as well by presenting relevant business and industry data that effectively makes the case for expedited change in the organization.

When leaders are effective at creating a sense of urgency, critical stakeholders understand and accept that organizational change must occur. They understand that the status quo is not acceptable and that the time for making change is running out. Why is urgency important to a change effort? Urgency is important because meaningful change cannot occur without the cooperation of the affected stakeholders. Therefore, creating a sense of urgency for a needed change is the first step leaders must take to gain the cooperation of others.

Leaders create a sense of urgency by both selling the value of a future state to stakeholders and making the status quo a dangerous place for them to remain. In effect, you and senior leaders create a compelling narrative that tells stakeholders why it is not in their best interest for the organization to stay in its current state.

This is often done through frank discussions about the current situations and competitive realities, sharing relevant information and data, and discussing opportunities and crises they may be facing.

Communication is critical and the communications about the urgent need for change must be honest. A manufactured sense of urgency will soon be seen for what it is, and this will doom a change effort to mediocrity.

ESTABLISH A LEADING ALLIANCE

One step you need to take to handle change is to establish a leading alliance. This is a series of actions that you take to identify capable, influential, and critical allies to become your change oversight team. Think about that step this way: now that a change leader has succeeded in gaining the attention of this talented and credible group, they now need to empower this high performing team to make the change happen. The keys to this step are first to identify the right people who can become committed partners with them through the change launch and its implementation.

Next, you must gain the willingness of the leading alliance to work with the change leader to bring about the actual organizational change desired. This is more than just assigning people to work on the change project as alliance members. When leaders are effective at establishing a leading alliance, they gain a high performing project leadership team whose members also believe and are committed to seeing the change occur.

Sometimes senior leaders make the mistake of believing that their superior power in an organization is all that it takes to make change happen. Power in every organization is distributed among all its stakeholders. Senior leaders who ignore the value of critical stakeholders will have minimal success with their change effort. Employees at all levels can sabotage a change initiative. Generally, change must be sponsored at the top of an organization, but it needs to be driven at the bottom and middle levels of an organization. For this reason, establishing a leading alliance is the critical component to the long-term viability of any change effort.

The next step is to develop a change vision and strategy. This is a series of actions to give a picture of what the future looks like after the change is implemented. This picture of what things can become is both a future that looks appealing and sensible. If it is not, then it will be hard for the leaders to sustain commitment to the effort. Here, leaders must maintain a balance between setting direction independently and collaborating with the leading alliance in this effort.

When leaders and the alliance are effective at developing a change vision and strategy, they will have identified the areas of change, provided clear and realistic targets for measuring success, and appealed to the long-term interests of organizational stakeholders. Senior leadership begins the change process by rallying to act. It does this again by creating a sense of urgency for a needed change, then develop that change vision and strategy. Sometimes this process can be rushed through too quickly but when done correctly, however, it requires time to get a change vision and strategy right.

COMMUNICATE THE CHANGE VISION

Continuing through the change process, it is imperative to communicate the change vision. This is a series of actions to communicate the vision broadly to promote understanding and commitment for the new direction. The goal here is to capture the minds and hearts of the employees and managers who are necessary to implement this change. With simple messaging that is repeated effectively in different formats, you can help others to both understand and accept the need for change.

Your goal in communicating the change vision is to make the complex simple. This sounds easy but often it is a difficult step for leaders to get right. Sometimes it is because they are used to telling rather than selling. Other times, it is because they are not good at getting their ideas across in a simple and understandable format. Good data is also critical in leading change, but don't let it become your enemy.

When you think about your own change communication message, do not let it become overloaded with facts, metrics, research studies, business trends, etc. All these information sources certainly have their place in your change effort, but they do not constitute the core messaging of your change vision.

Moving forward addressing change means you must empower broad based action. This is a series of actions to remove obstacles that do not support the change vision. At this point of the change journey, you are squarely in the implementation phase. You and the team are actively working with the rest of the organization to make changes to the existing infrastructure to put the wheels of change in motion.

When you and the team are effective at empowering broad-based actions, resistance to change is lessened and the existing infrastructure aligns more closely with the goals of the change effort. Empowering the broad-based action enters the difficult territory of the Devil is Always in the Details. Or, said another way, we can often agree that change is necessary. The problem occurs when we must agree on how to make that change happen.

GENERATE THE SHORT-TERM WINS

An overlooked and often minimized part of change, especially when focused on the big picture is looking at the small picture. A quote that I love says "take care of the small things and the big things will take care of themselves." That holds true here, where it is important to focus on and generate short-term wins. This is a series of actions to sustain the change effort over the long term by generating goodwill through visible short-term wins.

Consider this common outcome of change efforts: you and your team work hard to effect change but the difficulty of achieving complex goals eventually stalls momentum. When this occurs, the result is subpar change outcomes and frustration in the entire process. This can be bypassed by sustaining long-term momentum for their change efforts. The two ways to accomplish this are the following:

- Implement visible improvements in a shorter window of time
- Ensure that the improvements are clearly tied to the change effort

When you and the team are effective at generating short-term wins, you maintain the momentum for change that is critical to any successful change effort. If you have ever been involved in a large-scale change effort, you know how difficult implementing change can be. Change begins with good intentions but produce minimal results. As frustration, blame, and counter-blame spread in the aftermath of a failed change, change stakeholders are left with the burning question: What happened? Leaders retrace their actions; senior leaders can rightfully point to many things that they did well:

- They enthusiastically and forcefully identified the urgency of the needed change
- They created and empowered an effective leading alliance
- They communicated a compelling change vision

So, why does change that starts well still fall short in the long run? There can be many reasons for poor outcomes from a large-scale effort. Many times, however, failure comes from the lack of any early success. The truth is nothing dooms the momentum for a change initiative more than the lack of any evident and significant progress after a period of sustained effort. To sustain it over the long term, you must generate short-term wins. Without some early success, it is easy for stakeholders to believe that the effort is only wishful thinking.

CONSOLIDATE GAINS AND IMPLEMENT CHANGE

A series of actions to prevent the change effort from sliding into complacency and to continue momentum is to consolidate gains and implement change. This is where you must look beyond the low-hanging fruit of the short-term wins to tackle other projects in the change effort for implementation. First, this prevents you and the team from going back to its old way of doing things and second it combats continuing resistance to it.

When you are effective at consolidating gains and implementing more change you remove unnecessary processes, internal connections, and inter-departmental procedures that hinder the progress. Have you ever taken a long trip and passed some unfortunate traveler on the side of the road with a gas can in his hand, a non-responsive vehicle, and unhappy family members in the car? This scene is an accurate description of the state of some change efforts.

Like this family trip, many efforts run out of gas before the team ever reaches its desired goals. These efforts lose their momentum because of poor execution. Just like the traveler who overestimated how far the family could travel on a tank of gas, leaders overestimate how far their effort can proceed on the successful implementation of a few short-term wins. To avoid this fate, you and your guidance must consolidate the gains from earlier short-term wins and implement more change. You must reinforce the momentum.

ANCHOR CHANGE IN THE COMMUNITY

When you align yourself and your team with the new effort, you are essentially anchoring the change in the culture. The goal here is to take actions to ensure that the effort becomes firmly established and entrenched in every aspect of the functioning. As leaders, we make consequential adjustments to organizations' norms and values, human resource processes and procedures, reward programs, training and development, and other infrastructure areas to align these areas with the new directions all the time.

When you are effective at anchoring change in the culture, the effort becomes a lasting part of the culture and serves as a differentiator for you. Few outcomes are worse than devoting significant resources and time to substantial change efforts only to have things revert to its old way of doing things. These outcomes hurt morale and breed cynicism. It also makes others less committed to the next great initiative that wants to be sponsored. The failure to implement lasting change frequently occurs because leaders underestimate the difficulty of changing a culture.

NOTES:

CHAPTER 11

TELL THE STORY

"We tell ourselves stories in order to live." – Joan Didion

What is so special about us humans? After all, animals are also intelligent: we no longer believe that the ability to use tools or to recognize our reflection in the mirror is exclusively human. But, in all probability, we are the only species that can calm its young by telling them a princess coming back to life after being kissed by a frog. Only humans are helplessly drawn to stories, spending a fair share of our time in make-believe land, and in this chapter, you will find out why. You will learn about the many function's stories have for us and come to understand how they shape our lives even unconsciously.

OUR LIVES ARE FULL OF MAKE-BELIEVE STORES THAT REVOLVE AROUND TROUBLE

Whether you are aware of it or not, your brain spends a fair amount of its time far removed from real life. While you are at work, your mind is stretched out on faraway beaches. In the evening, for the ladies it is having a romantic dinner with Zac Efron while for the guys they are sitting across from Gisele Bundchen. On the weekend, it is waking up making sure we are clothed as we were literally just standing in our class during high school naked. These fantasies and dreams are all stories, and we are addicted to them. In fact, our lives are totally dominated by made-up stories. It is not just that we devour movies, TV shows and novels, we also encounter stories in the form of daydreams or even sports broadcasting.

Just think, for example, about the way typical pro-wrestling fights are staged. They look very much like theater plays, just with a little less reflection about life and a lot more violence. The memories of the "Heartbreak Kid" Shawn Michaels delivering the jaw dropping sweet chin music still bring me right back to my childhood. All of these followed simple story arcs with typical schemes and conflicts between the protagonist and antagonist, like who slept with whose wife, or who is the ultimate US patriot. These stories are not just something we consume. Rather, we are constantly spinning them ourselves. Indeed, we are excessive daydreamers. It is believed that we experience around a thousand daydreams per day, each lasting an average of about thirteen seconds. All in all, we dream away approximately four hours of every day.

Interestingly, these stories all tend to conform to the same structure, no matter where or how you encounter them. Put simply, a story is about a person who tries to overcome a problem, whether it is Mark Wahlberg playing another good guy overcoming a bunch of bad guys or John Wick constantly seeking vengeance for the killing of his dog given to him by his wife. In other words: stories tend to always revolve around trouble. After all, who would want to read a story about someone who spends his entire day lying on a sunny terrace, occasionally grabbing some food from the fridge, and drinking a pina-colada. While this may seem like a desirable way to live, it is a dull story. Trouble is just more interesting.

When it comes to the help of stories, we get to practice for real life. You probably enjoy food and sex. Evolution made these things enjoyable so that you would survive and procreate. But you probably like stories, too. So why would evolution make us crave stories? In a world where only the fittest survive, how do stories make us fitter? In part, it is because stories often have real-life applications. With the help of fictional stories, we can explore different ways to react to predicaments and gather experience without ever having to face the real-life consequences.

For instance, simply through imagining, you can experience to a certain degree how you would react if you encountered a bear named Bruno in the woods who was traveling from Wisconsin to Missouri, or what you would do stuck in the middle of a desert by Area 51 waiting on aliens to land. Think about it like a flight simulator: pilots use simulated cockpits to practice for real-life flights. Similarly, we practice real-life problems through stories. These simulations can also improve our social skills. Heavy fiction readers are believed to have better social skills than nonfiction readers. All the practice they get consuming fictional conflict makes them better at empathizing with others and settling strife.

You might be thinking that cannot be true. How can we possibly practice for real life by dealing with stories that are not even true? That is fair. However, even though we know the stories are made up, they still feel real to our brain. Scientists have conducted studies that proved this to be the case. In experiments, subjects had their brains scanned while they watched an old Western firm. Whenever the old Western actor seemed very angry or sad in the movie, the viewer's brain responded as if it, too, were angry or sad. As we can see, stories reproduce in the brain the same or similar sensations that we imagine the characters to have. We do not just perceive a story; we live it as if it were happening to us.

DREAMS ARE NIGHTTIME STORIES THAT HELP OUR BRAINS TO LEARN

Novels, movies, or a Netflix subscription can end up costing you a lot of money. But every single night you get a private screening of someone wrestling with bizarre and existential troubles for free. Even better: you get to be the story's main character. The common term, of course, for these nighttime stories is "dreams." Interestingly, dreams tend to follow a universal storytelling structure. Just like all good stories, your dreams focus on a hero or heroine, usually yourself, struggling to attain something. In other words: most dreams feature some sort of trouble.

It is believed that two-thirds of dreams involve at least one threat. In fact, the most common dreams are ones about being attacked or chased, followed by falling, drowning, and so on. Like other stories, dreams also serve to rehearse for real life. When you are dreaming, your brain does not know that what is going on is not real. For instance, if you dream that are drowning, your brain sends signals to your body telling you to try and hold your breath while swimming up for air. Luckily for us and those we share a bed with, evolution gave us atonia, or sleep paralysis, which keeps those signals from reaching the body and prevents us from acting out our dreams.

All the while that your brain is managing these dreamed-up conflicts, it is learning. The brain continues to form new connections while dreaming proving that fact. Even though we often forget our dreams, what we have learned is not lost. Rather, it is saved in the implicit or unconscious memory. This comes into that practice I mentioned earlier in the book, the "Captain and the Crew" that focuses on the conscious and subconscious mind. Unfortunately, while the knowledge is there, your conscious mind cannot access it. Only when we need it, for instance, in the face of perceived danger is when that knowledge seemingly pops out of nowhere.

Our mind weaves information into meaningful stories, and sometimes it goes awry. Let us face it: the world is a mess. So many things seem to happen without any rhyme or reason, and because we are human, we often struggle to accept this. Indeed, our mind is allergic to randomness, but addicted to meaning. For this reason, we are notoriously prone to weaving random information into stories to make sense of the world. When we give order to chaos, the world becomes easier to understand and cope with. You can think of your storytelling mind as a little Encyclopedia Brown. At the beginning of each story, Brown is faced with a puzzling adventure he must solve. But the complexity of that situation never deters him.

Brown keeps looking for clues until, eventually, there is enough information to make up a story that explains what happened, who was involved and why it came about. Like Brown, your mind is eager to find meaningful patterns in a world full of randomness and weave them into stories, thus closing explanatory gaps when phenomenally unlikely things happen. Sometimes, however, this need to make sense of the world is so powerful that our storytelling mind runs amok and constructs false explanations for events.

Conspiracy theories are a great example of this. These theories use real information to construct a coherent and satisfying story. Although these stories may be totally false, they nonetheless provide believers with simplistic yet reassuring "ultimate" answers. Conspiracy theories are not just the fantasies of lunatics. They are in fact quite popular among all classes and levels of education.

STORIES SHAPE OUR BELIEFS AND BEHAVIORS

It is said that good books can change your life. Even better, good stories can change nations. Stories have the power to provide identity and meaning to entire communities. They supply them with defining values, and thus serve as the glue that holds social lives together. But how do stories accomplish this? It all comes down to their good guy versus bad guy structure. Typically, stories feature a good guy, whose honesty and worth we will respect. Then there is a bad guy, who stands in opposition and whom we condemn. This structure spells out clear ideas of what is "good" and what is "bad," and can do so in ways that turn pre-existing social rules on their heads, which means that stories can be used to change the way people live.

Stories do a lot more than just tell us what is good and what is evil. In fact, fiction can have a major effect on our deepest morals and beliefs. The emotions conveyed in stories are contagious, and the more engaged we are when we consume a story, the more it affects our beliefs. For example, one study found that people who read a story about premarital sex being wrong were more likely to disapprove of the practice. Believe it or not, stories have an even greater influence on our thoughts and behavior than versus rational arguments.

When it comes to stories, everyone likes to tell the story of their life, but that is not necessarily a true story. William Shakespeare famously said that "all the world's a stage." And all your life is a story narrated in the first person, we may add. Alas, that narrative is not accurate. The story we tell of our lives is based on our memories. But our memories are highly flawed, meaning that our life stories often have little to do with the truth. Our memories do not provide us with picture-perfect records of every second of our lives. We tend to forget both fine details and major life events, and craft stories to fill the void.

For example, a study of people's memories of 9/11 found that 73 percent of subjects reported that they have vivid memories of the footage depicting the first plane crashing into the North Tower. However, this is simply impossible, as this footage was not available on the morning of the attacks. Not only are our life stories heavily embellished by totally fictional memories; we also tend to perceive ourselves as shining much brighter than we do.

After all, it is crucial to our identity that we are the good guys in our story. No one wants to be the bad guy. So, whenever we do something right, we make a big deal out of it; when we make a mistake, we either report it in a way that minimizes our culpability or leave it out of the story completely. We carry on by cultivating positive illusions about ourselves. For example, almost every driver estimates that they have above-average driving skills. Similarly, almost all university professors think they are better than average at their job. Obviously, neither of these is statistically possible. Curiously, the only people with reasonably accurate self-assessment capabilities are those who suffer from depression. As bizarre as it sounds, it seems we need unrealistically positive self-assessments to cope with our mundane and sometimes depressing world.

When was the last time you read a novel from beginning to end? Or went to a live theater performance? Or indulged in a poem? The habit of reading literature is going extinct, and some people believe that storytelling itself is vanishing with it. They could not be more wrong. Fiction is not dying. It just looks different today than it did before. While it is true that hardly anyone still reads poems, it is also true that we are constantly surrounded by poetry: the song lyrics we hear on the radio are essentially musical poetry.

In the future, stories will be consumed very differently. Just take the increasing popularity of massively multiplayer online role-playing games (MMORPGs) as an example. The MMORPG player actively takes part in the story by building a character, following a plot, and experiencing adventures themselves. Most notably, the player themselves can shape the story, thus making them essentially a co-author. It is likely that this is how we will experience many stories in the future: by acting them out ourselves in virtual worlds.

Clearly, stories are not going to disappear. In fact, the opposite is true: stories are becoming so ubiquitous that there is a real threat of over-consumption. One day, we might become lost in our fictional worlds. To understand how this might work, think about the way we deal with food nowadays. Food is so easily accessible and junk food is inexpensive that we run the risk of losing control, overeating, and damaging our health.

The same goes for stories: we could get so immersed in them that we lose touch with the real world. You have probably even experienced this yourself after binge-watching an eight-episode season of Jack Ryan or playing Fortnite for an entire day without even realizing it. As you have learned, stories are incredibly beneficial to individuals and communities. But only if you do not become addicted to them.

NOTES:

CHAPTER 12

CREATE A COMMUNITY

"You can please some of the people all of the time, you can please all of the people some of the time, but you can't please all of the people all of the time." – John Lydgate

Trying to reach everyone with your cause, like most people are still trying to do, only leads to mediocrity and a lack of intense feeling for your idea or brand. This chapter will show how anyone can form and build a community, and how to use this powerful force to change the status quo and create a new future.

WHETHER YOU KNOW IT OR NOT, YOU ARE ALREADY PART OF A COMMUNITY

For millions of years people have been part of a community. Whether the groups are religious, ethnic, or political, it seems we cannot help it: humans need to belong to a collective larger than themselves. In fact, cultures and communities are everywhere; and whether you know it or not, you also are a member of at least one of them, as an employee of your company, a member of your religious community or a fan of your favorite band.

But what is a community? All communities share three components: a group of people, a common cause and at least one leader who represents and organizes them. One of the most important features is the shared cause. A community shared cause leads its members to internalize the community's values and ideas as their own. These internalized incentives make the members into driven believers instead of mere followers. The cause of a community, either a yearning for or a resistance to change can be anything from environmental justice, a political campaign or a group of enthusiasts who believe in the superiority of their beloved products or services.

Communities have always been with us, but with today's technology, the number of them is exploding. This is mainly due to the internet: communities used to be local, but now, with the reach of the internet and especially social media geography is no longer a barrier to societal growth. And thanks to social media, their influence is no longer directly correlated to its size, but to the cause for which it stands, and how it uses communication technologies. Why? Because today, real sustainable growth derives from the people who truly love your cause, advocate your values and beats the social media drum for you.

Do not engineer your ideas for the masses: make it exclusive and meaningful for a distinct group of people. The marketing mantra of the past was to reach as many people as possible with your products or services. But times have changed. Many people are stuck in the past and still focus on developing products for the masses, a strategy which can lead to catastrophic consequences. The problem with creating a product or service that tries to please everyone is that almost every time, it leads to a mediocre product or service that people will use but not fall in love with.

Great influencers and companies are right to create an extraordinary product or service, because their community does not form around mediocre causes. People today are not content with off-the-shelf ideas anymore. A powerful cause needs to have a personal, exclusive, and meaningful story that people can identify with. Furthermore, it needs to scream of newness, and allow for people to be directly engaged in the movement. Fundamentally, a meaningful cause scratches an itch that has not been sufficiently scratched yet.

WITH TODAY'S TECHNOLOGY, EVERYONE CAN FORM AND LEAD A MOVEMENT

Be it a viral YouTube video or the latest ideas of influential TikToker's, reaching people has never been easier, cheaper, or more effective. So, what does this mean? You too can reach people by forming a new community. The first thing to know is that people need to be able to communicate intensely about their shared cause. This means that communication cannot just be vertical between you the leader and the individual members; more importantly, it must be horizontal, between all members.

And with today's technology, you have everything you need to facilitate both vertical and horizontal communication. Websites, blogs, and social networks allow you not only to spread your cause, but also provide the room and the tools for your community to communicate, share ideas and organize. For example, you can use Slack to organize projects, and Microsoft Teams to share brief updates about developments. At the same time, these websites allow you to set ground rules for participation and align everyone with your common vision by setting specific goals.

The reality is if you have a meaningful cause and the will to lead, people will follow. Have you ever wondered how many people make up a movement? The answer is around 1,000: that is the number of true believers you need for a group to keep moving. But how do you get so many people to follow your cause? You must tap into something people already yearn for. Creating a movement is about organizing an existing yearning into a way that community members can connect with each other and form a movement under your leadership.

A movement contains three elements: A narrative that tells the story of the future you're trying to build; a connection between the leader and the community and among the members; and something to do with the fewer limits, the better. But too often potential leaders do not realize that a movement cannot just be about money or themselves. If your cause is to be successful, it needs a meaningful story about something that is worth talking about. And too often, organizations only offer something to do and nothing to buzz about. So, what is the secret to creating a community? Tell a story to people who want to hear it. Help them connect as a community. Lead the movement. And finally, make a change.

FOCUS ON TIGHTENING CONNECTIONS IN THE COMMUNITY, NOT JUST GROWING IT

A bigger community is a better community, right? For most leaders, this sounds about right. But they are wrong. At least in the beginning, a community's biggest advantage is not its size, but the multiple connections between the members, the leader, and the outside world. In fact, a community has four different directions of communication: Leader to community, community to leader, community members to one another and community member to outsider. Normal marketing pales in comparison, with communication generally only in one direction: company to market. The most important of these directions is the communication between members. And this is where tightening a community comes in.

Tightening a community means bringing members closer together by facilitating communication and tightening their common bonds. You can do this by transforming a shared interest into one passionate goal, and by providing a platform for members to easily connect with each other. Or you can harness the power of insiders and outsiders. To create a feeling of cohesion, you must develop a culture of insiders – which inevitably excludes others. This allows the community to differentiate itself from other communities and create a stronger sense of internal identification. Remember, your main task as a leader is to organize and strengthen your community.

Management is primarily about getting a job done while leadership is about stepping into a vacuum and creating motion. For a community to form there must be a change that people want to see made. This need for change must come from a certain discomfort with the status quo, from a sense that there is something missing in the world. A leader steps right into this discomfort zone, the vacuum and starts to organize so people will follow them. Here is a quote I came up with and tell my daughters every time they find themselves in position of discomfort, "make the uncomfortable comfortable."

Leaders do this despite the risks because of two things: they have faith in the cause, and they know that innovation is always more effective the earlier it happens, so the sooner the better. But with all this talk about leaders you might be thinking well, that is fine for the famous and the charismatic; but that is not me. How can I be a leader? You can do this by correcting your misconceptions.

The truth is leaders are first generous and through that are charismatic. Many people today have the impression that you must be famous or ooze charisma to be a leader. But in fact, people and that means potential community members very quickly sniff out whether your motivation is authentic and altruistic, or if you are just an egomaniac. Real leaders are generous and more focused on giving than taking. They believe in the inherent value of their cause, and therefore make others believe in them.

To make the world a better place, we need more dissenters and less sheep-walkers. We have seen how rewarding being a community leader can be. So why isn't everyone doing it? The answer is simple. There are too many sheep-walkers out there, people who have been conditioned by school and community to be obedient and afraid of change. They have been taught to keep their heads down and mind their own business, just like sheep. Well-educated sheep, but sheep, nonetheless.

What we need in the world are more dissenters, people who question the status quo and the existing dogmas and act without asking for permission. Organizations need more dissenters to advocate change from the inside: because if you hire amazing people and give them freedom, they will do amazing things. And communities need dissenters as leaders to break into new territory and help change the world.

So why aren't there more dissenters out there? Because the media primes us with a story about dissenters: one filled with tales of inevitable downfalls and self-delusion. After all, who would dare believe they can challenge the status quo? You can overcome this false narrative by talking yourself out of the fear: remind yourself that everything worth doing is risky, and that the world needs and demands the change you are trying to make. Fear is what is stopping us from transforming our ideas into reality and changing the status quo. But with today's technology, there is no excuse anymore: you no longer need power or money to make a change. So, step up and start leading your own community.

NOTES:

CHAPTER 13

BRAND YOURSELF

"The question isn't, 'What do we want to know about people?', It's, 'What do people want to tell about themselves?'" – Mark Zuckerberg

Who do you want to buy stuff from a brand, or a person? These days, social media makes it easier than ever for brands to connect with customers. But people have a natural aversion to being sold to by faceless, impersonal people or brands that are clearly just hanging out on social media with no clear direction. Social media will only help you if you are sociable, relatable, and not too explicit about your desperate desire for marketing and reliability. A more indirect approach to selling yourself, your service, or your product will yield better results in the long term.

That is not to say that there is not a manner of smart tactics you can use to hack your way to social media success. But whatever you do, you must not lose sight of the need to humanize your brand.

IN THE NEW ERA OF SOCIAL MEDIA, TRADITIONAL MARKETING IS ON LIFE SUPPORT

Marketing is everywhere. Turn on the TV, browse the internet and everywhere you go, you will see ads, paid for by marketing budgets. But when was the last time you saw an ad for something, and decided to buy it? Now think about this. When was the last time you bought something like a song, some clothes, or a pair of sunglasses because it was recommended to you by friends or people you follow online? Maybe it just happened to "pop-up" on your news feed. Chances are, it was recently. And if people have not noticed this trend already, they need to start doing it right now.

OK, so you want to sell your product or service. The obvious, traditional approach is to make a load of ads, in print and online, which forcefully tell people to "Buy it now." But that sort of aggressive messaging turns people off: nobody likes a hard sell. What that means is, your goal should not be to "market." It should be to get people talking to each other about you and your brand. The truth is people buy from other people. And social media is an unbelievably good way to get them to do this.

The fact of the matter is that being sold to, at least if it is done right can be a thing of beauty. Some of the best marketers I have come across are people who I follow on multiple social media platforms, from LinkedIn to Twitter to Facebook. I interact with these marketers to get to know them, become a part of their life in a sense and they only try to sell me stuff when they know the time is right. Social media marketing needs a personal touch, that element of real human connection. It is not about having millions of followers, especially not on Facebook, where only around 1 percent of the people who "like" your page will see a post organically. Rather, it is about engaging people, getting them talking, getting to know them.

Traditional marketing is always talking, never listening. Social media can be more effective because it is more flexible, more personal, and, more social, as the name suggests. But only if you do it well. We will explore how to do that more as we continue here.

Bad social media posts can feel a bit like being left alone on an island as if you are yelling and yelling, but nobody is listening to you. It might feel like even a volleyball would be great company like Tom Hanks and Wilson in "Castaway". But the thing is, you are not really on your own. People are all around you. You just need to work out how to engage them. How do you do that? How do you get people to engage with your brand on social media, so you do not end up chatting away to inanimate sporting goods? The answer is to be more human.

One quick way is to ask your followers questions. Questions like "What's the best thing you've bought recently?" or "If you were President, what is the first thing you would change" might sound basic and they are but they still spark a conversation, which is the most important thing. You can also try sharing interesting facts or tips that relate to your product and educate people as well as keeping them entertained. Whatever you do to get people's attention, you need to follow up on it too, in other words, you need to be social. That means not signing off after you post, but rather checking back and engaging with people's replies to you and thanking them for responding and answering their questions.

You should also back up your posts by going under the radar. As soon as you post something, it is worth telling people about it via DM (Direct Message). You can also set up exclusive groups or group chats for people you know appreciate your work, known as engagement pods. This should ensure that your post circulates widely. Plus, getting early interactions will make the social network's algorithm think that your post is popular, which will further boost its reach. This applies especially to Facebook.

You also need to bring an analytical approach to every part of the process. That means not just measuring the success of posts, but also deciding which platforms to post to in the first place. Maintaining a social media presence is a lot of work, so you should only invest your time in the platforms your target demographic uses. Otherwise, you might as well be talking to that volleyball.

THE KEY TO A SUCCESSFUL ONLINE PRESENCE IS PERSONALITY

Social media is full of opportunities for you and your brand to express your personality. So, you need to hunt them out.

You should search through social networks like Twitter and Instagram for mentions of your hashtags you follow or your brand, even the ones you are not tagged in. In other words, you should find out what people are saying about you behind your digital back. You can even follow what people are saying about your competitors.

You can absolutely make an impact by creating fresh, relatable content that your target audience wants to see. For more serious-minded companies, the key is education. Think about what people want to know about you, your brand, your business, or whatever else, and find a fun and relatable way to share that information with them. Brands need to work hard to create online personalities that feel human. Individuals, meanwhile, need to build up a well-defined personal brand. Across multiple platforms including LinkedIn, Facebook, YouTube, and Snapchat, you can create content that is all about your experience at any point of time in your life and it can even be very personal content that really resonated with people and could eventually help establish you as an expert in your field.

Rather than chasing after vanity metrics, do whatever it takes to grow engagement organically. Do you want a million Facebook "likes?" Guaranteed retweets or YouTube subscribers? A spot on the coveted Instagram Explore page at the stroke of a button. There are ways to get these in no time at all if you are willing to pay. And a lot of people do, because they are hung up on what are called vanity metrics, things like number of followers and total reposts.

Essentially, that is cheating. But there is a bigger problem with this tactic, beyond the fact that it is underhanded. Basically, if you simply purchase a bucketload of Facebook "likes," those users will not actually be interested in your product which means they will not engage with you. That is why cheating does not work. Not only will you be wasting your money with this approach you will be wasting a ton of time, effort, and energy as well because of how social media algorithms work. I could write an entire book just expanding on this chapter, but you will have to trust me.

The classic example of a vanity metric is follower count. A high count looks great on a PowerPoint slide and might be enough to convince colleagues that your social campaigns are going well. That is why so many people cheat to get high follower counts with ease. But as a strategy for growing your actual brand, this is useless. Because it does not lead to genuine engagement. Think about it: who are those hundreds of thousands of new followers you have just bought? It is pretty much certain that they will not actually be interested in your brand and they might even be bots rather than real people. So, they will barely notice when you post, they will not engage with your content and they certainly will not end up becoming customers.

Rather than vanity metrics, then, you need to stay focused on building up engagement. You need to find an audience that is not just big but is also actually interested in your product. There are still plenty of ways you can do this through exploiting how social networks operate. This growth is called chopping. Basically, it means anything goes, so long as it stops short of cheating. And remember, rather than aiming for "likes" or follows, you are trying to capture people's attention, in the form of engagement.

Facebook Groups are one great way to do it. How about setting up a group for superfans of the sort of thing you sell? Facebook Watch Parties are also worth exploring: this lesser-known feature brings people together at the same time, giving you a great shot at going viral. Of course, metrics are important to keep track of how you are doing.

But only worry about the right ones. Engagement is a far more valuable metric than follower count. Even better is what is called "ROE:" return on engagement. After all, your goal through all of this is still to grow your business.

YOUR MOST POWERFUL ADVOCATES ARE THE ONES YOU ALREADY HAVE

By now you know that your priority on social media should be to humanize your brand content. Here is a radical idea. If you need to humanize your brand content, why not enlist those people who already know and love what you do? Whether it be friends, family, or employees, you probably already have a far broader social media presence than you realize. That is because so many of your people will be using social media every day anyway and they would be willing to help you out, if you asked.

When it comes to employees, you can harness your employees' social media presence by launching an employee advocate program. Invite your staff to join it, and before you know it, you'll have a huge raft of new social media advocates, all of whom know about your brand, and in fact make a living from it.

You can provide resources for them through a content hub which there are several very useful ones to select online. That way everyone has a script they can use as well as some basic guidelines. But you cannot tell them exactly what to do because it is important, they must be themselves. Your job will be to keep an eye on how they do and reward your most talented storytellers with extra opportunities such as a takeover of your main account. Do not forget about your customers, too. Seeking out, interacting with, and shouting about positive mentions of your brand is always a great idea. And just like with employees, you should try to inspire a sense of loyalty and community.

Of course, none of this means that the days of the social media professionals are numbered though it will change the way they do their jobs. Brands will eventually need to bring their key content creators in-house, as the importance of great storytelling becomes ever clearer. Expect to see a shift toward faces, rather than logos, representing brands simply because they are more engaging. Another change will be that chief marketing officers will give way to chief digital officers. Just in case you did not already believe that traditional marketing is on life support.

Technology is changing everything fast and social media is so powerful but there will always be the human touch. Even with artificial intelligence coming at us fast as well. In fact, it is already arrived. Social media managers can already benefit from plenty of automated tools, for everything from following and unfollowing, to automatically sending out DMs. Messenger bots on Facebook, though far from perfect, are a great place to start experimenting with this technology. But the most important change, for every brand right now, is to become more human, not less.

Make no mistake: social media is here to stay. Many people have predicted the demise of Facebook recently, especially in the wake of the latest scandals. But they are not going anywhere. In fact, Facebook is one of the greatest, most transformative inventions in human history. Like the other major social networks, it is changed everything. Facebook itself is changing, though, and not just because of AI. As a company driven by profit, it is always going to keep making alterations that affect how it can be used for commercial purposes.

If you want to excel as a social media expert, you will need to be able to adapt quickly to changes and work out how to leverage them to your advantage. Other social networks, meanwhile, come and go, although those such as Instagram and LinkedIn are mainstays. It is worth watching emerging platforms including TikTok and YouTube's forthcoming Short too. These platforms may all play a big role as Millennials start to grey and Generation Z assumes the hot seat. I am personally interested to see with the young generations how platforms such as Twitch come into play in addition to just gaming.

Of course, each platform requires its own type of content, and its own tactics for success. But some points hold true in general for good social media practice. Most importantly, no brand should lose sight of the fact that people use social media for fun to relax, and, of course, to socialize. And that is why your brand needs to be as human as possible. Traditional marketing may be on life support, but your brand does not have to be. Humanize your brand, and, whatever the future holds, your business can be a part of it.

.

NOTES:

ABOUT THE AUTHOR

Nick Jarman is a servant leader focused on providing exceptional insights and actionable solutions to engage, inspire, and empower. His focus is on getting individuals and organizations from where they are to where they need to be. He focuses on the five pillars of success: Mindset, Purpose, Caring, Communication, and Courage. Nick provides leadership coaching and corporate consulting services. For more information about Nick visit his website at www.nickmjarman.com

CONNECT WITH NICK

Nick would love the opportunity to connect with you and has strategically set up a structure to do just that. For Nick, his passion is serving others to engage, inspire, and empower them. The best way he can accomplish this is to connect with you. Feel free to reach out to him by any of the methods below:

Text: (636) 233-9779

Email: nickmjarman@gmail.com

Facebook: @nickmjarman (*note the m*)

All other social media platforms: @nickjarman

Social media icons designed by Sophia Jarman

This book is dedicated to my wife Joani, my daughters Isabella, Abigail, Sophia and my mom.